WORLD MYTHOLOGIES SERIES

GODS
&
PHARAOHS
from
EGYPTIAN
MYTHOLOGY

NUT

GODS
&
PHARAOHS
from
EGYPTIAN MYTHOLOGY

TEXT BY GERALDINE HARRIS
COLOUR ILLUSTRATIONS BY DAVID O'CONNOR
LINE DRAWINGS BY JOHN SIBBICK

SCHOCKEN BOOKS

NEW YORK

DOUGLAS &
McINTYRE

VANCOUVER/TORONTO

HATHOR

SHU

RA-KHEPRI

GEB

WATERS OF CHAOS

Copyright © 1982 by Eurobook
Limited
Published by agreement with
Eurobook Limited, London
First American edition published
by Schocken Books 1983

10 9 8 7 6 5 4 3 2 1   83 84 85 86

**Library of Congress Catalog-
ing in Publication Data**
Harris, Geraldine.
  Gods and pharaohs from
  Egyptian mythology.
  (World mythologies series)
  Includes index.
  1. Mythology, Egyptian.
  2. Gods, Egyptian.
  I. Title. II. Series.
  BL2441.2.H37
  1983   299′.31   82-5519

Published in Canada by
Douglas & McIntyre Ltd.
1615 Venables Street
Vancouver, British Columbia

**Canadian Cataloguing in Pub-
lication Data**
Harris, Geraldine.
  Gods & pharaohs from
  Egyptian mythology
  (World mythologies)
  Originally published:London:
  P. Lowe, 1982.
  Includes index.
  ISBN 0-88894-387-3
  1. Mythology, Egyptian—
  Juvenile literature.
  I. O'Connor, David. II. Title.
  III. Series.
  PZ8.1.H376 Go 1983
  j.299′31   C83-091065-4

Printed in Great Britain by
William Collins, Glasgow

ISBN 0-8052-3858-1
(Schocken)
ISSN 0732-2291
ISBN 0-88894-387-3
(Douglas & McIntyre)

Contents

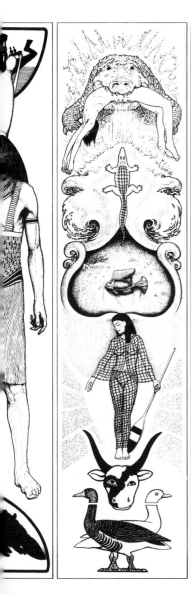

Red land, black land

For centuries Europeans have been fascinated by ancient Egypt. When the Emperor Napoleon invaded Egypt in 1798 he took with him a team of scholars to examine and record pyramids, obelisks and other ancient monuments. It was one of Napoleon's soldiers who found the famous Rosetta Stone on which the same royal inscription was written once in Greek and twice in Egyptian in two different scripts. In 1822, with the help of the Rosetta Stone, the brilliant young French scholar, Jean Champollion, was able to decipher the ancient Egyptian hieroglyphic script and gave a voice to the past.

Throughout the nineteenth century, scholars travelled all over Egypt to make drawings of temples and tombs and to record inscriptions. These early drawings are often very valuable since so much has been damaged or destroyed in the last hundred years. The early excavators however were little better than treasure hunters; their main concern was to find spectacular objects or well-preserved mummies to take back to European museums. Gradually the importance of methodical excavation was realized and excavators acknowledged that a piece of broken pottery or a scrap of papyrus might be more significant than a gold vase because of the information it could give about ancient Egypt.

In the middle of the nineteenth century the French scholar, Auguste Mariette, entered the service of the Khedive of Egypt and founded the Cairo Museum and The Egyptian Antiquities Service, which still has the task of protecting all ancient sites and carrying out excavations. It was Mariette who in 1881 became suspicious of the large number of ancient royal jewels that were suddenly appearing on the market. He soon discovered that a family from the village of Qurna had found a burial chamber filled with the mummified bodies of some of the greatest rulers of ancient Egypt. In 1898 more royal mummies were found in a tomb in the famous Valley of the Kings and it is now possible to visit the Cairo Museum and gaze on the very faces of the men who ruled Egypt over three thousand years ago.

It was not only the French who excavated in Egypt. The Egypt Exploration Fund, founded in London in 1882, financed numerous expeditions and the British archaeologist W.M.F. Petrie, who worked in Egypt and Palestine for sixty years, set new standards in the excavation and description of ancient sites. It was also a British team who made the most famous archaeological discovery of the twentieth century. In 1922, after many years of work in the Valley of the Kings, Howard Carter found the almost intact burial of a pharaoh of the fourteenth century BC. The treasure of Tutankhamon aroused tremendous popular interest in Egyptology. Since that date expeditions from all over the world have worked to recover Egypt's magnificent past.

Many of the distinctive features of Egyptian civilization can be traced to the country's unusual geography. Egypt is a place of contrasts and the greatest contrast of all is between the 'red land' of the desert and the 'black land' of the lush Nile valley. In very ancient times the Egyptian desert was covered in grass and inhabited by vast herds of animals, like the savannahs of modern Africa. The first Egyptians were hunters, following the herds of game. Then the climate became drier, the savannah shrivelled into desert and the people came down from the uplands to live in the Nile valley and turn its swamps into rich agricultural land.

The skies of ancient Egypt were a clear, brilliant blue and rain was almost unheard of. Only the presence of the river Nile, with its annual flood, made it possible to grow crops. The flood, which brought fertile mud from higher up the river, could be partly controlled by dykes and canals, but there was a limit to what men could do to extend the agricultural land. In the south the habitable land remained a narrow strip on either side of the river; all the rest was desert. In the north the Nile splits up into many branches before reaching the Mediterranean Sea. Much of the fertile land in the Delta was too marshy to be cultivated but it was rich in birds and fish, papyrus plants for paper-making and reeds for hut- and boat-building. The marshes and the numerous waterways made it difficult to travel across the Delta but in the south the single broad river ensured easy communications, especially as boats could sail upstream with the prevailing wind behind them or float downstream with the current. The people of the north sailed the Mediterranean, traded with other Near Eastern countries and were open to

foreign influence. The people of the south, sealed off from the world by the surrounding deserts, were more conservative and had a stronger sense of unity.

To begin with, every small Egyptian settlement or tribal area had its own chieftain, but gradually leaders arose who claimed authority over whole groups of settlements. By the fourth millenium BC some of these leaders were calling themselves kings and their kingdoms grew larger and larger. The ancient Egyptians believed that a man called Menes had once ruled over the south (the Kingdom of Upper Egypt) and had fought a war against the north (the Kingdom of Lower Egypt). In about three thousand BC the south conquered the north and Menes ruled the whole country from his new capital, Memphis.

The Egyptians grouped their rulers into dynasties and counted Menes as the first king of Dynasty One. Modern historians divide the thirty dynasties who ruled over an independent Egypt into seven main periods. The most important of these were the Old Kingdom (c2575–2134 BC), the age of the pyramid builders; the Middle Kingdom (c2040–1640 BC) when the country was reunited by another leader from the south, and the New Kingdom (c1550–1070 BC) when Egypt ruled an empire under pharaohs such as Tutankhamon and Ramesses the Great. In between the 'Kingdoms' came times of political chaos. Foreign invaders occasionally caused havoc and because Upper and Lower Egypt were different in character there was always a danger that under a weak ruler they would split apart again.

Egypt was never able to forget that it had once been two countries. The ruler was always called the Lord of the Two Lands, the King of Upper and Lower Egypt. He wore a double crown made up of the White Crown of Upper Egypt and the Red Crown of Lower Egypt and was often shown protected by The Two Ladies, Nekhbet, the vulture goddess of the south and Wadjet, the cobra goddess of the north.

One thing that did unite all the Egyptians was a reverence for kingship. The king was sacred, the living image of the Sun God himself. Much of a king's time was spent in complex religious

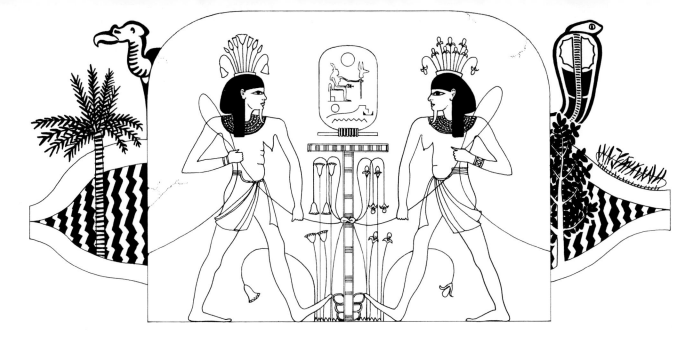

rituals but he was also the active head of government. As absolute ruler his power was enormous but he was meant to use it only for the good of his people. At his coronation an Egyptian king re-enacted the events of creation and promised to conquer chaos and establish *Maat*.

Maat means order and justice and truth and it was personified by a goddess who was the daughter of the Sun God. Kings were supposed to 'live in truth', rule with impartial justice and make Egyptian society reflect the divine order established by the gods. Because kings were thought to be more than human they could stand between mankind and the gods and ask for peace and prosperity for all Egypt.

Some deities were worshipped throughout the country but every part of Egypt had its local god or goddess. Many of these deities embodied the principal characteristics of animals and could be shown in animal or animal-headed form. So the god Khnum, the giver of life, was represented as a vigorous ram or with a ram's head, the goddess Taweret, protector of women in childbirth, had the paws of a lion, the back of a crocodile and the bulky body of a hippopotamus, while the complex nature of the goddess Hathor was expressed in a variety of forms from ferocious lioness to benevolent cow.

A very large number of gods and goddesses were revered in ancient Egypt but behind this diversity lay the idea that all gods were really one. Egyptian texts often simply refer to God but the mysterious power of the Sole Creator was illustrated by giving him numerous divine forms, male and female, beautiful and terrible, fierce and gentle. The ordinary person focused his worship on the forms that were most appropriate to his own life, or on his local god or goddess.

These local deities might achieve national importance if they became the patrons of a dynasty of kings. It was one of the king's chief duties to build temples as houses for the gods and to make daily offerings to them. In return for these offerings the gods were expected to give the king life, health and the power to overcome his enemies. If a king reigned for thirty years he celebrated a *Sed* Festival. During this festival the king went through days of complex rites to win the blessing of renewed life and strength. Everything had to be done twice, once for Upper and once for Lower Egypt and in one of the most important ceremonies the king ran round and round a specially built track. This may have been meant to prove that he was still fit enough to rule as the living image of the Sun God and in very ancient times a king who failed to run the whole course was probably ritually murdered.

For most of Egyptian history, however, the king was allowed to die a natural death. It was thought to be important to the whole country that the dead king was accepted by the gods into an afterlife, to triumph over death just as the sun triumphed over darkness with each new dawn.

Because of this idea the burial rites of an Egyptian king were costly and complex and their most spectacular feature was the erection of a pyramid.

When Egypt was first united, houses, palaces and shrines were built with reeds or in mud-brick, but as early as the Third Dynasty (c2649–2575 BC), Imhotep, the first great architect in history, designed a stone step pyramid for the burial of his master, King Zoser. By the Fourth Dynasty (c2575–2456 BC) the Egyptians were building huge straight-sided pyramids in the desert near Memphis.

The largest of these, the pyramid of King Khufu at Giza, is one-hundred and forty-six metres high and contains about two million, three-hundred-thousand blocks of stone, each weighing between two and fifteen tons. In spite of their vast size the pyramids of Giza are built with extraordinary precision. We cannot be certain how they were constructed but it is clear that simple copper tools and simple methods were used. The Egyptians were not great technical innovators but they had a genius for organization and no shortage of manpower and time.

A king began work on his pyramid as soon as he came to the throne. About four thousand craftsmen were employed to cut and shape blocks of good limestone and fit them together. Getting the blocks from the limestone quarries to the site of the pyramid took up most of the manpower. Once cut, the blocks were loaded onto barges and floated downriver until they were level with Giza. Then they were offloaded, placed on wooden sledges and dragged along a log-causeway to the pyramid site. The final stage was to haul the blocks up the earthen ramps that surrounded a half-built pyramid to the place where they were needed.

It is wrong to think that the pyramids were built by gangs of slaves toiling under the lash. The main workforce was the agricultural population, who had nothing to do for three to four months of every year while the fields were flooded. As many as a hundred-thousand men may have worked together to move vast quantities of stone and build a pyramid for their divine king.

The Great Pyramid is now much the same colour as the desert in which it stands, but when it was first built it was cased in gleaming white limestone and had a gilded capstone. Attached to the pyramid were two temples, linked by a walled causeway, and in a nearby pit a full-size boat was buried for the king's use in the afterlife. After the king's body had been embalmed it was taken to the first temple, The Valley Temple, which contained twenty-three royal statues. The mummy was purified and a ritual was performed to give life to the king's statues so that his spirit could inhabit them as if they were his human body. Then the royal coffin was dragged along the causeway to the second temple where further ceremonies were performed and where priests would continue to make offerings to the king's spirit for centuries after his death. Finally the coffin was taken down a narrow passage into the heart of the pyramid and laid in a stone sarcophagus in the burial chamber.

In the pyramids of the Fifth and Sixth Dynasties (c2465–2152 BC), texts are inscribed on the inner walls and these may be the words recited by the priests during the royal burial. The Pyramid Texts vary in age and character. Some are humble prayers that the king might join the gods as their servant; others are far more arrogant. In the so-called 'Cannibal Hymn' the dead king is said to be so powerful that he can kill and eat the gods to absorb their magic: 'The large gods for his morning meal, the medium ones for his evening meal, the little ones for his supper and the old ones for the fuel under his cooking pot.'

When the rites were over the priests withdrew, lowering a series of huge stones to block the route to the burial chamber. In spite of these precautions, no intact royal burial has been found in the pyramids of the Old Kingdom.

Thieves were able to break in and steal the precious objects buried with the kings, but the pyramids themselves remained to become the greatest of the Seven Wonders of the Ancient World and the only one of those wonders to have survived to our own day.

Archaeologists are not only concerned with gods and kings and a great deal has been discovered about the daily lives of ordinary people in Ancient Egypt. Most of our evidence for daily life comes from the New Kingdom (c1550–1070 BC) and one of the best sources is the village of Deir el-Medina in southern Egypt. During the New Kingdom royalty were buried in large rock-cut tombs in desert valleys close to the city of Thebes, the religious capital of the south. The government built a village for the craftsmen who cut and decorated the royal tombs at nearby Deir el-Medina.

The craftsmen lived with their wives and children in mud-brick houses fronting the narrow streets of a walled village. When the houses were first built they were all identical but the families who lived in them soon changed that by knocking down internal walls, building extensions and decorating the rooms with wall-paintings. In many of the houses the front room was used as a workshop.

The second room was the largest and was raised above the level of the rest of the house on a column made from a palm-tree trunk. It had unglazed windows and a mud-brick platform on which the master and mistress of the house sat. There would have been little other furniture; chairs were for the rich and the important but folding stools and low wooden tables were used. Behind the main room there was often a small bedroom. Egyptian beds had wooden frames, webbing of woven reeds and high footboards. They were made up with linen sheets but a padded wooden headrest was used instead of a pillow. Close to the bed stood chests, painted to look like costly ivory and ebony, which held clothes, jewellery and make-up.

During the New Kingdom, Egyptian clothes were usually made from cunningly draped and pleated linen. Women's clinging dresses and men's long kilts and wide-sleeved shirts were white. Colour was added by brilliant bead collars and bracelets and by the garlands of real flowers worn on festive occasions. Hairstyles could be very elaborate and wigs of dyed wool were sometimes worn. Both men and women used eye make-up and a typical Egyptian cosmetic chest might contain a mirror, razor and tweezers in copper, a pot of rouge, lip-paint, green eye-shadow, black eye-liner and jars of the scented oils that the Egyptians loved to rub on their bodies.

None of the Deir el-Medina houses had the luxury of a bathroom and the passage beside the bedroom led to an open kitchen area. The main items of kitchen equipment were a domed, terracotta oven, a grindstone for the grain which formed a major part of the craftsmen's wages, and cooking pots of every shape and size. Bread and beer made up the bulk of an Egyptian's diet and a small rock-cut cellar behind the kitchen area would have contained jars of beer and perhaps some date wine. Dates or honey were used to make sweet bread and cakes and the Egyptians also enjoyed figs and pomegranates, grapes and water-melons. Beef and roast goose were highly prized but most people only ate meat on special occasions. The protein in their diet was provided by dried fish, lentils and peas. Other common vegetables were leeks, onions, garlic and cucumbers.

A staircase from the kitchen area led up to the roof where vegetables were spread out to dry and animals such as geese or goats might be kept.

The Egyptians were very fond of animals and are often shown with pet dogs, cats or monkeys.

In hot weather people slept on the roof and it was also a place to sit playing a board game or gossiping to the neighbours. From their rooftops the people of Deir el-Medina could look out at their ancestral tombs, built on the slopes above the village and at their local temple. Every house had its own little shrine where daily offerings of wine and bread and flowers were made to the statue of a favourite deity. Some houses had wall-paintings of the goddess Taweret and Bes, the lion-headed dwarf god, who in spite of his fierce and ugly appearance was the much loved protector of women and young children. Bes and Taweret were also carved on beds and headrests to guard sleepers against snakes and scorpions and all dangers of the night, and small images of these deities were often worn as charms, called amulets.

The Egyptians had great faith in the magical power of amulets. Nearly all Egyptian jewellery is made up of amulets and every Egyptian wore them for protection from the cradle to the grave. Hundreds of different shapes were used but the most popular were miniature images of the gods or of divine symbols such as the falcon-eye of the god Horus, the pillar of the god Osiris or the cow-eared human face of Hathor. The gods were not only to be found in the great temples, they were part of daily life and they dominate the stories told and loved by the Egyptians.

The waters of chaos

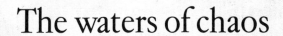

Egyptian religion was richer in symbols than in myths, but some of
the gods did have stories attached to them. Unfortunately, because
they were so well known, many of these stories were never written
down in full. Often a myth has to be pieced together from scattered
references to it in hymns and prayers, temple inscriptions, Pyramid
Texts and even odder sources such as spells for curing scorpion bites.
Many ancient Greek writers were fascinated by the deities of Egypt
and recorded myths about them, but it's difficult to know how close
these versions are to the original Egyptian stories.

Some myths, such as the murder and resurrection of Osiris, were
often re-enacted during royal ceremonials or temple rites. Scholar-
priests in great religious centres like the Temple of Ra at Heliopolis,
the Temple of Ptah of Memphis or the Temple of Thoth at
Hermopolis produced cycles of myths with their own deity as the
central figure. All these cycles included creation myths because to the
Egyptians, creation was the only important event in history. The
whole aim of their society was to preserve the divine order
established by the Creator and the idea of progress had no place in
Egyptian thought. A dozen different myths were not enough to
express the marvel of creation. The Creator had many forms and
many names—Ra, Ra-Atum, Amon-Ra, Ra-Horakhty—but all the
sources agree that he first arose out of a watery abyss called Nun.

In the beginning were the waters of chaos. Darkness and silence

reigned but in the depths of the watery abyss lay the formless spirit of the Creator, the father and mother of all things. . . . One story tells how a mound of earth slowly rose above the waters of Chaos, just as Egypt seems to rise up as the Nile floods sink in the heat of summer. This mound was the first land and at last there was a place in which the spirit of the Creator could take on a body. In the form of a phoenix with flaming plumage the Creator alighted on the Primeval Mound and his cry shattered the eternal silence with the first sound.

A second story tells how eight creatures with the heads of frogs and serpents moved through the waters of chaos before time began. They were the Ogdoad: Nun and Nunet, deities of the watery abyss, Heh and Hehet, deities of infinite space, Kek and Keket, deities of darkness and Amon and Amonet, deities of invisibility. These mysterious beings swam together to form the great egg that was to hatch the Creator.

Others said that this Primeval Egg was laid on the risen mound by a goose whose cackling was the first of all sounds. The Great Cackler sat on the mound guarding her egg through countless ages until at last it hatched into a shining phoenix. The two halves of the shell separated the waters of chaos and formed a space in which the Creator could make the world.

A third story tells how darkness covered the waters until the Primeval Lotus rose from the Abyss. Slowly the blue lotus opened its petals to reveal a young god sitting in its golden heart. A sweet perfume drifted across the waters and light streamed from the body of the Divine Child to banish universal darkness.

This child was the Creator, the Sun God, the source of all life but every evening a lotus sinks below the surface and does not rise again until dawn. So the Primeval Lotus closed its petals at the end of each day and vanished back into the waters. Chaos reigned through the night until the god within the lotus returned. The forces of chaos were not conquered for ever at the beginning of time, they surrounded the earth in the form of serpents poised to attack the Sun God. The war between Order and Chaos will never end.

Whatever the form of the Creator, all the stories agree that even when he lay in the watery abyss he knew that he was alone. This solitude became unbearable and he longed for other beings to share the new world with him. In Memphis the priests described how the thoughts of the Creator became the gods and everything else which exists. When his thoughts had shaped them, his tongue gave them life by naming them. Thoughts and words were the power behind creation.

In Heliopolis the priests named the Creator as Ra-Atum and told how after aeons of solitude he spat out Shu, the god of air and Tefenet, the goddess of moisture. For a great span of time Ra-Atum was still alone for Shu and Tefenet were lost to him in the waters of chaos. Then the Creator took an eye from his face and filled it with his power. He called the Eye his daughter, Hathor, and sent her out into the darkness to search for his lost children.

The light of the Eye pierced the forces of chaos and Shu and Tefenet were quickly found and brought back to their father. As a reward, the Sun God set the Eye on his forehead in the form of a great cobra, the uraeus serpent. He promised her that she would have power over his enemies and that in ages to come both gods and men would fear her.

Then Ra-Atum embraced his first children, Shu and Tefenet, with tears of joy. As he held them in his arms, his spirit went into them and they and all the gods to come shared in the divinity of the Creator.

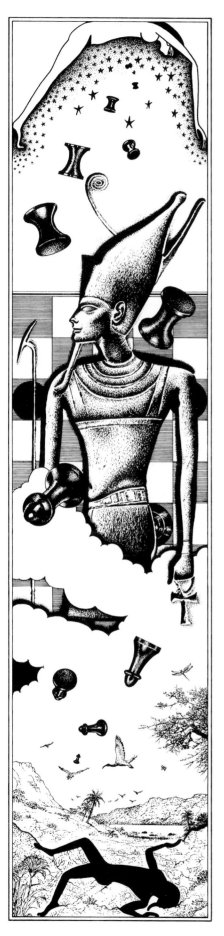

The nine gods

Shu and Tefenet, the first children of Ra-Atum, loved each other and in time Tefenet gave birth to twins. The elder twin was Geb, the god of the earth and the younger was Nut, the goddess of the sky. Geb loved his sister, the beautiful Nut, and for many ages they embraced each other. The sky pressed against the earth and there was no space between them for anything to live and grow.

Finally Ra-Atum became jealous of the great love of Nut for Geb and he ordered their father Shu to separate them. The mighty god of the air trampled Geb beneath his feet. Then he lifted Nut on the palms of his hands and held her high above her brother. Although Nut was pregnant, Ra-Atum laid a curse on her so that she could not give birth on any day of the year. Geb struggled beneath his father's feet and Nut leaned down but they could not reach each other.

Meanwhile the Creator had given life to many other beings and among these was Thoth, the wisest of the gods. Thoth looked up at the beautiful body of Nut arching above the world and he loved and pitied her. He decided to help the unhappy goddess and at once invented the game of draughts. Thoth challenged the gods to play against him with time as the stake. Gradually the wise god was able to win enough time to make up five days. The length of the year had been fixed by the Creator at three hundred and sixty days but Thoth added the time that he had won to make five extra days. These days did not lie under the curse of Ra-Atum so Nut was at last able to give birth to her children.

On the first day she bore a child who was already crowned and he was called Osiris. On the second day came Haroeris and on the third, after a great deal of pain, Seth. The fourth and fifth days saw the birth of two daughters, Isis and Nephthys. Osiris and Isis had fallen in love in their mother's womb and became husband and wife. Seth and Nephthys were also married eventually but there was never any love between them.

The two daughters of Nut were different in character; Isis was brave and cunning, the Mistress of Magic, wiser than millions of men while Nephthys was loyal and gentle. The brothers Osiris and Seth were even more different. Osiris was handsome, noble and generous. Seth had the head of a savage beast and it betrayed his nature, for he

was greedy and cruel and could never forgive Osiris for being the elder brother and destined for kingship.

Ra-Atum, with Shu and Tefenet his children, Geb and Nut his grandchildren and Osiris and Isis, Seth and Nephthys his great-grandchildren were honoured as the nine great gods under the name of the Ennead. Many other gods and goddesses were called into existence by the Creator and he filled the sky above the earth and the sky below it with spirits and demons and lesser deities.

Last of all he created Man. Some said that mankind had sprung from the tears of joy wept by Ra-Atum when Shu and Tefenet were brought to him through the waters of chaos. Others told how the first man had been formed by Khnum, the ram-headed god, on his potter's wheel. When the Creator had breathed life into his new creatures he made a land for them to live in, the kingdom of Egypt.

Ra-Atum protected Egypt with barriers of desert but he created the river Nile so that its waters would flood the land and rich crops would grow. Then he made the other countries and for them he put a Nile in the sky, which we call rain. Ra called the seasons and the months into being and clothed the earth with trees and herbs and flowers. Finally he made every kind of insect and fish, bird and animal and gave them the breath of life.

Each day Ra-Atum walked through his kingdom or sailed across the sky in the Boat of Millions of Years. Whenever they saw the sun all the living creatures in Egypt rejoiced and praised their Creator. To hold back the forces of chaos and to champion order and justice, Ra-Atum invented kingship. He himself became the first and greatest King of Egypt and ruled for countless centuries in joy and peace.

The secret name of Ra

Ra, the Sole Creator was visible to the people of Egypt as the disc of the sun, but they knew him in many other forms. He could appear as a crowned man, a falcon or a man with a falcon's head and, as the scarab beetle pushes a round ball of dung in front of it, the Egyptians pictured Ra as a scarab pushing the sun across the sky. In caverns deep below the earth were hidden another seventy-five forms of Ra; mysterious beings with mummified bodies and heads consisting of birds or snakes, feathers or flowers. The names of Ra were as numerous as his forms; he was the Shining One, The Hidden One, The Renewer of the Earth, The Wind in the Souls, The Exalted One, but there was one name of the Sun God which had not been spoken since time began. To know this secret name of Ra was to have power over him and over the world that he had created.

Isis longed for such a power. She had dreamed that one day she would have a marvellous falcon-headed son called Horus and she wanted the throne of Ra to give to her child. Isis was the Mistress of Magic, wiser than millions of men, but she knew that nothing in creation was powerful enough to harm its creator. Her only chance was to turn the power of Ra against himself and at last Isis thought of a cruel and cunning plan. Every day the Sun God walked through his kingdom, attended by a crowd of spirits and lesser deities, but Ra was growing old. His eyes were dim, his step no longer firm and he had even begun to drivel.

One morning Isis mingled with a group of minor goddesses and followed behind the King of the Gods. She watched the face of Ra until she saw his saliva drip onto a clod of earth. When she was sure that no-one was taking any notice of her, she scooped up the earth and carried it away. Isis mixed the earth with the saliva of Ra to form clay and modelled a wicked-looking serpent. Through the hours of darkness she whispered spells over the clay serpent as it lay lifeless in her hands. Then the cunning goddess carried it to a crossroads on the route which the Sun God always took. She hid the serpent in the long grass and returned to her palace.

The next day Ra came walking through his kingdom with the spirits and lesser deities crowding behind him. When he approached the crossroads, the spells of Isis began to work and the clay serpent quivered into life. As the Sun God passed, it bit him in the ankle and crumbled back into earth. Ra gave a scream that was heard through all creation.

His jaws chattered and his limbs shook as the poison flooded through him like a rising Nile. 'I have been wounded by something deadly,' whispered Ra. 'I know that in my heart, though my eyes cannot see it. Whatever it was, I, the Lord of Creation, did not make it. I am sure that none of you would have done such a terrible thing to me, but I have never felt such pain! How can this have happened to me? I am the Sole Creator, the child of the watery abyss. I am the god with a thousand names, but my secret name was only spoken once, before time began. Then it was hidden in my body so that no-one should ever learn it and be able to work spells against me. Yet as I walked through my kingdom something struck at me and now my heart is on fire and my limbs shake. Send for the Ennead! Send for my children! They are wise in magic and their knowledge pierces heaven.'

Messengers hurried to the great gods and from the four pillars of the world came the Ennead: Shu and Tefenet, Geb and Nut, Seth and Osiris, Isis and Nephthys. Envoys travelled the land and the sky and the watery abyss to summon all the deities created by Ra. From the marshes came frog-headed Heket, Wadjet the cobra goddess and the fearsome god, crocodile-headed Sobek. From the deserts came fiery Selkis, the scorpion goddess, Anubis the jackal, the guardian of the dead and Nekhbet the vulture goddess. From the cities of the north came warlike Neith, gentle cat-headed Bastet, fierce lion-headed Sekhmet and Ptah the god of crafts. From the cities of the south came Onuris, the divine huntsman and ram-headed Khnum with Anukis his wife and Satis his daughter. Cunning Thoth and wise Seshat, goddess of writing; virile Min and snake-headed Renenutet, goddess of the harvest, kindly Meskhenet and monstrous Taweret, goddesses of birth—all of them were summoned to the side of Ra.

The gods and goddesses gathered around the Sun God, weeping and wailing, afraid that he was going to die. Isis stood among them beating her breast and pretending to be as distressed and bewildered as all the other frightened deities. 'Father of All,' she began, 'whatever is the matter? Has some snake bitten you? Has some wretched creature dared to strike at his Creator? Few of the gods can compare with me in wisdom and I am the Mistress of Magic. If you will let me help you, I'm sure that I can cure you.'

Ra was grateful to Isis and told her all that had happened. 'Now I am colder than water and hotter than fire,' complained the Sun God. 'My eyes darken. I cannot see the sky and my body is soaked by the sweat of fever.'
'Tell me your full name,' said cunning Isis. 'Then I can use it in my spells. Without that knowledge the greatest of magicians cannot help you.'
'I am the maker of heaven and earth,' said Ra. 'I made the heights and the depths, I set horizons at east and west and established the gods in their glory. When I open my eyes it is light; when I close them it is dark. The mighty Nile floods at my command. The gods do not know my true name but I am the maker of time, the giver of festivals. I spark the fire of life. At dawn I rise as Khepri, the scarab and sail across the sky in the Boat of Millions of Years. At noon I blaze in the heavens as Ra and at evening I am Ra-atum, the setting sun.'
'We know all that,' said Isis. 'If I am to find a spell to drive out this poison, I will have to use your secret name. Say your name and live.'
'My secret name was given to me so that I could sit at ease,' moaned Ra, 'and fear no living creature. How can I give it away?'

Isis said nothing and knelt beside the Sun God while his pain mounted. When it became unbearable, Ra ordered the other gods to stand back while he whispered his secret name to Isis. 'Now the power of the secret name has passed from my heart to your heart,' said Ra wearily. 'In time you can give it to your son, but warn him never to betray the secret!'

Isis nodded and began to chant a great spell that drove the poison out of the limbs of Ra and he rose up stronger than before. The Sun God returned to the Boat of Millions of Years and Isis shouted for joy at the success of her plan. She knew now that one day Horus her son would sit on the throne of Egypt and wield the power of Ra.

The Eye of the Sun

Hathor, the daughter of Ra had many forms. She could be a cow or a cat and she came to newborn children to foretell their fate in the form of seven beautiful women. Hathor in human form was the most gracious and joyful of goddesses but when she took on the role of the Eye of the Sun, she could also be the fiercest and the cruellest. She was the protector of the gods but when she was angry even the gods feared her. Temple inscriptions and a story written in Egyptian as late as the second century AD tell of a grim time when Hathor left her country and chose to live in Nubia.

The Eye of the Sun was jealous of the other gods and goddesses whom Ra had created. She quarrelled with her father and wandered south to roam the deserts of distant Nubia. The angry goddess abandoned her lovely human form and appeared as a wildcat or a raging lioness. She lived by hunting and butchered every creature who came near her.

Egypt was desolate, for without beautiful Hathor laughter and love withered away and life held no joy. The Sun God hid his face in sorrow and gloom spread across the earth. No-one could console him for the loss of his beloved daughter and worst of all without the power of his Eye, Ra was in danger from his enemies. Darkness tightened its coils around Light and Chaos threatened Order. 'Who will bring Hathor back to me?' asked Ra but the gods were silent. The Eye of the Sun held the power of life or death over all beings and in her furious mood the gods were afraid to approach her. Then Ra summoned Thoth, the wisest of deities, and ordered him to go to Nubia and persuade Hathor to return to Egypt. Thoth obeyed the King of the Gods with a heavy heart. He was sure that if Hathor recognized him she would kill him before he had a chance to speak. With this in mind, Thoth transformed himself into a humble baboon. Then he crept through the Nubian desert, following the bloody trail of the goddess.

When he found her, Hathor was in her wildcat form, sitting on a rock licking her tawny fur. Thoth crawled forward, knocking his head on the ground:

'Hail, daughter of the Sun!' he said humbly.

Hathor arched and spat but when she saw that it was only a baboon she paused and did not spring on him at once. 'Gracious goddess,' faltered Thoth, 'may a humble ape dare to speak to you?'

'Speak and die,' growled the wildcat as she unsheathed her claws. The baboon cringed and kissed the ground, murmuring, 'O, powerful one, if you choose to kill me, I cannot stop you but remember the story of the mother vulture and the mother cat. . . .'

'What story?' demanded Hathor.

'Listen my lady,' said wiley Thoth, 'and I will tell you.'

The wildcat sat down and began to wash herself again. She seemed to take no further notice of the baboon but Thoth knew that if he tried to run away he would feel her claws within seconds. He began his story.

There was once a female vulture, who made a nest in a palm tree and sat on her eggs until four fine chicks were hatched. As soon as they broke through their shells the chicks demanded food, but the vulture was afraid to leave her nest because of a wildcat who lived on a nearby hillside. Now the wildcat had given birth to four kittens and she was just as afraid to leave them, because of the vulture.

The chicks and the kittens were soon crying with hunger so the two mothers came together and arranged a truce. The vulture and the wildcat both swore a mighty oath by Ra that neither of them would attack the other's children. Then the vulture felt safe to fly off and look for carrion and the wildcat felt safe to go hunting.

For some weeks everything went well and the chicks and the kittens thrived. The young vultures were soon trying out their wings and the kittens began to play all over the hillside. One morning while the vulture was circling over the desert, the boldest of her chicks flew out of the nest. His wings were not yet strong and after a short flight he landed on the hillside where the kittens were playing and snatched away a piece of their food.

Quicker than thought, the wildcat struck at the young vulture and wounded him badly. 'Find your own food,' growled the wildcat. The young vulture feebly flapped his wings but he found that he could not fly.

'Now I shall never return to my nest,' he gasped, 'but you have broken your oath and Ra will avenge me.'

When the mother vulture arrived at the nest with a beak full of carrion flesh, she found that one of her chicks was missing and saw him lying dead on the hillside.

'So the cat has broken her oath,' thought the vulture. 'I shan't wait long to have my revenge.'

The next time that the wildcat went off to hunt, the vulture swooped down on the kittens. She killed every one of them and carried them back to her nest to feed her chicks.

When the cat returned with her catch, the kittens were nowhere to be seen. She searched the whole hillside mewing desperately but all she found were a few bloodstained tufts of fur. Then she knew that the vulture had killed her kittens and she cried to Ra for vengeance: 'O great god who judges between the just and the wicked, the vulture has broken her holy oath and murdered my children! Hear me Ra and punish the oath-breaker!'

The Sun God listened to her prayer and was angry that an oath sworn in his name had been broken. Because the vulture had taken her own vengeance and killed all the kittens, Ra ordered a divine messenger to arrange her punishment.

The next day when the vulture was flying over the desert searching for food she saw a lone huntsman cooking a haunch of meat over his campfire. The vulture swooped down, seized the meat in her claws and carried it triumphantly back to her nest. There she dropped it amongst her greedy chicks but a few glowing embers still clung to the underside of the meat. As soon as the embers touched the dry twigs and grass of the nest it burst into flames. The three chicks were burned to cinders while their mother circled helplessly overhead. The wildcat ran to the foot of the blazing tree and called up to the vulture, 'By Ra, you killed my kittens but now your chicks are dead and I am avenged!'

'So my lady,' concluded Thoth, 'both the mothers had broken their oaths and both were punished. Ra hears and sees everything and punishes every crime. Praise to Ra who gives life to all things and whose shining face brings the whole earth joy. The Nile rises to make him a cloak. The north wind and the south wind blow at his command when he crosses the sky above and the sky below. He rules from the heights of heaven to the depths of the ocean. Praise to the Sun God and praise to Hathor his daughter.'

The goddess sat thinking over the story and remembering her just and powerful father. Thoth saw his opportunity and crept closer. 'My lady, I bring you divine food from the palace of the Sun God. Wonderful herbs that give health and joy to whoever tastes them.'

He held out the bunch of herbs in one paw and their sweet scent tempted the wildcat to nibble at them. As she swallowed the divine food, Hathor's mood changed. All her anger melted away and she listened meekly to Thoth. 'These herbs were grown in Egypt,' said Thoth, 'the land that rose from the waters of Nun, the place shaped for gods and men by the Creator, the home of Ra, your beloved father and Shu your dear brother. Is there a single living creature who does not long for the country of their birth?' asked Thoth. 'Even rocks and plants cling to their native soil. Animals live close to the burrows where they were born and as for mankind, Fate allows his favourites to live and die and be buried in the place of their birth. What more could anyone desire and how can anyone live happily or rest in peace in a foreign land?'

While she raged in the desert, Hathor had forgotten her home and her family but the words of Thoth brought back her memory. She thought of her father and her brother and remembered all the temples where men had honoured her as the greatest of goddesses. Suddenly Hathor was overwhelmed by a longing for Egypt and her tears were like a cloudburst.

Thoth watched her cry for a while and then said softly, 'O my lady, now you are grieving for your home but think of the flood of tears that Egypt has shed for you. Without you, the temples are empty and silent. Without you there is no music or dancing, no laughter or drunkenness. Without you, young and old despair but if you come back with me now harps and tambourines, lutes and cymbals will sound again. Egypt will dance, Egypt will sing, the Two Lands will rejoice as never before. Come with me, come home and I will tell you another

story as we travel north. Once upon a time a hawk, a vulture and a cuckoo all met together . . .'

Thoth bounded forward, confident that Hathor would follow, but the goddess suddenly realized that all along the baboon had been trying to lure her back to Egypt. She was furious that he had made her weep and with a terrible roar she turned herself into a huge lioness. Her pelt was the colour of blood and crackled and smoked like a living flame. Her face shone brighter than the disc of the sun and her fiery glance terrified Thoth. He jumped like a grasshopper, he shivered like a frog, he saluted her as if she was the glorious sun itself. 'O, powerful one have mercy! I beg you in the name of Ra to spare me! Gracious goddess, before you strike listen to the story of the two vultures!'

Hathor's anger cooled a little and she was curious to hear the story, so she changed back into a wildcat. Thoth began hastily to speak.

Two vultures once lived amongst the desert hills. One day the first vulture boasted, 'My eyes are sharper than yours and my sight is keener. No other winged creature has a gift like mine.' 'And what is this gift?' asked the second vulture. 'By day or by night I can see to the ends of the

The first vulture lifted his bald head and looked beyond the desert to the shores of the distant sea. 'The falcon has been swallowed by a fish with the snake still caught in its claws. Now the first fish is being eaten by a larger fish.' The vulture was silent for a minute and then spoke again. 'Now the big fish has swum too close to the shore and a lion has scooped it out with his paw. He's making a meal of the fish . . . Ah!' The first vulture ruffled his feathers and sidled along the branch in excitement. 'A griffin! A griffin has just swept down and carried off the lion to its nest!'

'Are you sure? Can it really be true?' asked the second bird.

'If you don't believe me, fly with me to the griffin's nest,' said the first vulture, 'and see for yourself!'

So the two vultures took off from the branch and flew across the desert hills till they were close to the lair of the griffin.

'See,' whispered the first vulture, 'his head is like a falcon's and his eyes like those of a man. He has the body of a lion and his ears are like the fins of a fish and his tail like a serpent.' The two birds watched the griffin tearing the last strips of flesh from the lion's bones and then flew away to a safer place.

'Everything that we have seen shows the power of Ra at work in the world,' began the first vulture. 'Even the death of a fly is noticed by the Sun God and those who kill will be killed, violence is repaid by violence. Yet, strangely, nothing has happened to the griffin, although he ate the lion.'

'That must be because the griffin is the messenger of Ra,' answered the second vulture. 'The Sun God has given him the power of life or death over all creatures. There is nothing stronger than the griffin except the justice of Ra.'

'So my lady, it is your father who repays good with good and evil with evil,' concluded Thoth. 'And he has filled you with his power. You are the Eye of the Sun, his avenger.'

The heart of Hathor beat with a fierce joy and she was proud again to be the daughter of the Sun God.

'Stop trembling. I won't kill you now,' promised the wildcat. 'Your words have bewitched me,

earth,' answered the first bird. 'High in the sky or deep in the ocean, I can see everything that happens.'

'It may be true that your eyes are sharper than mine and that your sight is keener,' agreed the other vulture, 'but my ears are sharper than yours and my hearing is keener. I can listen to every sound from land and sky and sea. I can even hear the voice of Ra as he decrees the fate of all creatures on earth.'

The two birds spent many days arguing over whose gift was the more precious, but one morning as they sat together on the branch of a dead tree the second vulture began to laugh. 'What are you laughing at?' demanded his companion.

'I am laughing at the way the hunter can so quickly become the hunted,' said the second vulture. 'A bird on the other side of the sky is telling me what he's just seen. *You* would never be able to hear him at such a distance. He saw a fly caught and eaten by a lizard. A moment later the lizard was seized and swallowed by a snake and the moment after that the snake was snatched up by a hungry falcon. It proved too heavy and the falcon and the snake have both fallen into the sea. If your sight is so good, tell me what's happened to them.'

yet I know that you mean me no harm. You have driven away my grief and anger.'

'My lady, if you will follow me,' began Thoth timidly, 'I will lead you back to Egypt. It isn't many days journey across these hills.'

'Then let us set out at once, at once,' growled Hathor, 'and no more chattering.'

The baboon began to walk towards Egypt with the wildcat a few paces behind him. Thoth was still afraid that she might change her mind, or lose her temper again so he began another story.

Two jackals lived in the desert and were devoted friends. They hunted as a pair and always ate and drank together and shared the same patch of shade. One day as they rested beneath the branches of a desert tree they saw an angry lion bounding towards them. The two jackals stood quite still and let the lion reach them. He was puzzled by this and roared out, 'Are your limbs stiff with age? Didn't you see me coming? Why haven't you run away?'

'Lord Lion,' answered the jackals, 'We saw you coming in your fury and we decided not to run. You would have overtaken us anyway and why should we tire ourselves out before being eaten?'

Since the powerful are not angry with truth, the lion was amused by this cool answer and he let the two jackals go.

'I have told you nothing but the truth,' said Thoth, 'and now that you have spared my life we can travel to Egypt together and I will protect you.'

'You protect *me*? The Eye of the Sun needs no protection from a baboon.'

'The strong can sometimes be saved by the weak,' answered Thoth. 'Remember the story of the lion and the mouse.'

'What story is that?' asked Hathor and Thoth told it to her as they walked towards Egypt.

Once upon a time there was a lion who lived in the desert hills. He was so huge and strong and fierce that all the other animals feared him. Now one day this lion came across a panther who was lying on the ground more dead than alive. The panther's fur had been torn out and he was bleeding from deep cuts all over his body. The lion was amazed, because he thought that only he was strong enough to get the better of a panther.

'What happened?' he demanded. 'Who has done this to you?'

'It was Man,' sighed the panther. 'There is no-one more cunning than Man. May you never fall into his hands!'

The lion had never heard of a beast called Man but he was angry that any creature should inflict such cruel wounds merely for amusement. He decided to hunt down Man and set off in the direction from which the panther had come. At the end of an hour's walk the lion met a mule and a horse who were yoked together, with metal bits hurting their tender mouths.

'Who has done this to you?' asked the lion.

'It was Man, our master,' said the horse.

'Then is Man stronger than both of you?'

'Lord Lion,' answered the mule, 'there is no-one more cunning than Man, may you never fall into his hands!'

Then the lion was angry again and more determined than ever to find and kill this cruel creature called Man. He walked on and soon met an ox and a cow roped together. Their horns had been sawn off and metal rings pierced their tender noses. When the lion asked who had done such a thing he received the same answer: 'It was Man, our master. There is no-one more cunning than Man, may you never fall into his hands!'

The lion set off again and the next thing he saw was a huge bear lumbering towards him. As he came closer, the lion noticed that the claws and teeth of the bear were missing.

'Who has done this to you?' he asked. 'Surely Man cannot be stronger than you?'

'It is true,' groaned the bear, 'for Man is more cunning. I captured Man and made him serve me, but he said to me "Master, your claws are so long it is difficult for you to pick up food, and your teeth are so long that it is difficult for you to get the food into your mouth. Let me trim your nails and your teeth and then you will be able to eat twice as much food." I believed him and let him do as he asked but he pulled out my claws and filed away my teeth. Then he was no longer afraid of me. He threw sand in my eyes and ran away laughing.'

After hearing this the lion was angrier than ever and ran on until he came across another lion with its paw caught in the trunk of a palm-tree.

'What's happened here?' asked the first lion. 'Who has done this to you?'

'It was Man,' growled the second lion. 'Beware of him, never trust him! Man is evil. I made Man my servant and asked him what work he could do, for he looked such a feeble creature. He claimed that he could make an amulet that would give me immortal life. "Follow me," said Man, "and I will turn this tree into an amulet. Do exactly as I say and you will live forever!" So I went with Man to this palm-tree and he sawed a slit in the trunk and wedged it open. He told me to put my paw inside and I did. The next thing I knew, Man had pulled out the wedge. The cleft closed on my paw and I couldn't get it free. Man threw sand in my eyes and ran away laughing and now I am trapped here till I starve to death.'

Then the first lion roared a challenge: 'Man! I will hunt you down and make you suffer all the pain that you have inflicted on other creatures!'

He bounded on until he noticed a small mouse in his path. He raised one paw to crush it but the mouse squeaked out, 'O Lord Lion, don't crush me! I'd hardly make you a mouthful, you wouldn't even taste me. Give me the breath of life and one day I may be able to return the gift. Spare me now and I will help you when you are in trouble.'

The lion laughed. 'What could a tiny mouse ever do to help the strongest of all beasts? Besides, no-one has the power to harm me.' 'Lord Lion, the weak can sometimes help the strong,' insisted the mouse and he swore a great oath to be the lion's friend. The lion thought this very funny but because it was true that the mouse was not worth eating, he let it go.

Now Man had heard the lion roaring and set traps for him. He dug a pit, spread a strong net of leather thongs across the pit and covered both with grass. That evening the lion came bounding along, looking for Man and he fell in the pit and was caught fast in the net. For hours he struggled to free himself, but in vain. By midnight the great lion lay exhausted, waiting for dawn and for Man to come and kill him. Suddenly a voice close to his ear squeaked, 'Lord Lion, do you remember me? I am the mouse whose life you spared and now I have come to save you. What is more beautiful than a good deed repaid?'

The little mouse began to gnaw at the leather thongs. For hour after hour he worked to set the lion free and just before dawn he bit through the last thong. The lion leaped up and shook himself free of the net. With the mouse clinging to his mane, the lion jumped out of the pit and ran away from Man, back to the desert hills. Fate had taught him that every power will one day meet its master and that the weak can help the strong.

Hathor understood the moral of Thoth's story and she followed the baboon with new respect but she seemed in no hurry to get back to Egypt. When they reached the edge of the desert she lingered under the date-palms and the sycamore-figs and the carob trees, praising their fruit. The baboon climbed the trees, hoping for a glimpse of Egypt. He tried the fruit and found it good, but he reminded the goddess that the fruit of the trees of Egypt was even better, so they went on together.

When they crossed the border the people of Egypt flocked to honour the returning goddess. At el-Kab she appeared to them as a vulture and in the next town as a gazelle but when they were close to Thebes she turned herself back into a wildcat. Before entering the city they lay down to rest. Hathor fell asleep and Thoth watched over her.

The enemies of Ra were angry that the Eye of the Sun had returned to Egypt. Under cover of night a chaos serpent crept towards the sleeping goddess, hoping to poison her and rob Ra of his protector. Vigilant Thoth saw the serpent poised to strike and woke Hathor. The wildcat leaped on the serpent and broke its back. She was grateful to the baboon for his warning and remembered the story of the mouse who saved the lion.

The next morning they entered Thebes and the city went wild with joy. A great feast was given in the temple of Mut, a feast that went on for seven days with eating and drinking, music and dancing and laughter. Hathor was so pleased that she changed from a wildcat into a lovely and gentle woman. Then she let the baboon lead her north again.

At the holy city of Heliopolis, Ra was reunited with his daughter and when they embraced the whole land leaped for joy. A feast was held in the House of the Sycamore at Memphis and all the gods and goddesses celebrated the return of Hathor. Then Thoth changed back to his usual form and Hathor recognized him at last. He sat down beside her at the feast and Ra gave thanks for the cunning of Thoth who had brought home the Eye of the Sun.

The anger of Ra

On the walls of royal tombs and on the golden shrine that protected the mummy of Tutankhamon, was inscribed 'The Book of the Divine Cow', a book which told the story of how the anger of the Sun God nearly destroyed mankind . . .

Ra was old and his bones were like silver, his skin like burnished gold and his hair like lapis-lazuli. When the people of Egypt saw how old and frail their king had become they murmured against him and the murmurs grew into plots to seize the throne of Ra. The plotters met in secret on the edge of the desert and thought themselves safe but as the Sun God watched over Egypt he saw the traitors and listened to their plotting.

Ra was so sad that he longed to sink back into the watery abyss but he was also more angry than he had ever been before. He spoke to the followers who stood about his throne: 'Summon my daughter, the Eye of Ra; send for mighty Shu and Tefenet; bring their children Geb and Nut; fetch the dark Ogdoad, the Eight who were with me in the watery abyss; raise Nun himself! But let them all come here secretly. If the traitors hear that I have summoned a council of the gods they will guess that they have been discovered and try to escape their punishment.'

The followers of Ra hurried to obey him. The message was taken to the great gods and goddesses and one by one they slipped into the palace. Bowing before the throne of Ra, they begged to know why they had been summoned with such haste and secrecy. Then the King of the Gods spoke to Nun, the Lord of the watery abyss and to the other deities: 'O oldest of living things and all you primeval gods, I wept and men sprang up from my tears. I gave them life but now they are tired of my rule and they plot against me. Tell me, what should I do to them? I will not destroy the children of my tears until I have heard your wise advice.'

Watery Nun spoke first. 'My son, you are older than your father, greater than the god who created you. May you rule forever! Both gods and men fear the terrible power of the Eye of the Sun; send it against the rebels.'

Ra looked out over Egypt and said, 'The plotters have already fled deep into the desert. They are afraid that I will learn about their plans and punish them. How shall I pursue them?'

Then all the gods cried out with one voice: 'Send the Eye of Ra to catch them! Send the Eye of the Sun to slaughter them! All of mankind is guilty, let the Eye go down as Hathor and destroy the children of your tears. Let not one remain alive.'

Hathor, the Eye of the Sun, most beautiful and terrible of goddesses, bowed before the throne and Ra nodded his head. Hathor went down into the desert, raging like a lioness. The plotters scattered this way and that but none of them escaped her. She siezed them and slaughtered them and drank their blood. Then merciless Hathor left the desert and raged through villages and towns, killing every man, woman and child she could find. Ra heard the prayers and screams of the dying and began to feel sorry for the children of his tears, but he remained silent.

When it was dark, Hathor returned triumphantly to her father. 'Welcome in peace,' said Ra. He tried to calm the fury of his daughter but Hathor had tasted the blood of men and found it sweet. She was eager for the morning when she could return to Egypt and complete the slaughter of mankind to avenge their treachery. Soon the power of Ra would be unquestioned, but he would have no subjects to rule.

The Sun God wondered how he could save the rest of mankind from his terrible daughter without going back on his royal word. Soon he had thought of a plan. Ra ordered his followers to run, swifter than shadows, to the city of Abu and bring back all the ochre they could find there. As soon as they had returned with baskets full of red soil he sent them out again to fetch the High Priest of Ra from Heliopolis and all the slave-girls who worked in his temple. Ra ordered the High Priest to pound the ochre to make a red dye and set the slave-girls to brewing beer. The High Priest pounded until his arms ached and the slave-girls worked desperately all through the night to brew seven thousand jars of beer. Just before dawn the red dye was mixed with the beer until it looked like fresh blood. The King of the Gods smiled. 'With this sleeping potion I can save mankind from my daughter,'
he said. 'The people have suffered enough.'

Then Ra had the jars carried to the place where Hathor would begin her killing and ordered the beer to be poured out to flood the fields with crimson.

As soon as it was light, Hathor came down into Egypt to sniff out and slaughter the few who were left alive. The first thing she saw was a great pool of blood. The goddess waded into it and was enchanted by her own reflection in the crimson surface. She stooped to lap up the blood and liked it so much that she drank the pool dry.

The beer was strong and the goddess soon became very happy. Her head whirled and she could not remember why she had been sent down to Egypt. Pleasantly drowsy, Hathor made her unsteady way back to the palace of Ra and sank down at her father's feet to sleep for many days.

'Welcome, gentle Hathor,' said Ra gravely. 'Mankind shall remember their escape from your fury by drinking strong beer at all your festivals.' The men and women who were left did remember and always afterwards Hathor was known as The Lady of Drunkenness. At her festivals the people of Egypt could get as drunk as they liked in honour of the goddess and nobody would blame them.

But Ra was still angry and sad about the rebellion of mankind. Nothing could be the same as it had been in the golden age before their treachery. When Hathor finally woke, she felt as she had never felt before and Ra said, 'Does your head ache? Do your cheeks burn? Do you feel ill?' As he spoke, illness first came into being in Egypt.

Then Ra summoned a second council of the gods and said, 'My heart is too sad and weary for me to remain as King in Egypt. I am weak and old, let me sink back into the watery abyss until it is time for me to be born again.'

Nun said quickly, 'Shu, protect your father, Nut carry him on your back.'
'How can I carry the mighty King of the Gods?' asked gentle Nut, and Nun told her to turn herself into a cow. Then Nut was transformed into a huge cow with golden flanks and long curved horns. Ra mounted the Divine Cow and rode away from Egypt.

The murder of Osiris

When the Sun God decided to leave Egypt the people who had escaped the fury of Hathor were angry and afraid. As the earth darkened everyone blamed his neighbour. Men made the first weapons and attacked anyone who might be an enemy of the Sun God. Ra looked back and knew that from that time onwards, man would always kill man in Egypt. He spoke sadly to the Divine Cow: 'Take me where I can still see mankind, but far out of their reach.'

Then the body of the Divine Cow became the sky, arching over the earth and Ra made the stars and scattered them along the belly of Nut. Next the King of the Gods made the Field of Peace and the Field of Reeds as homes for the blessed dead. By then Nut had begun to tremble because she stood so high above the earth. So Ra created the Heh gods, the Twilight Ones, to support her and he commanded airy Shu to stand between the earth and the sky.

Next Ra summoned Thoth and said to him, 'See, I will shine here in heaven and I will light the sky above and the sky below. You must represent me on earth and record the deeds of men.' Then he created the ibis form of Thoth and made him the keeper of records.

When Ra was lighting the undersky the earth was in darkness and men were afraid and wept for the loss of the Sun God. Ra heard them and also transformed Thoth into the Great White Baboon. Thoth shone with a silvery light and mankind no longer dreaded the sinking of the sun because Ra had created the moon. So ibis-headed Thoth was the wise Scribe of the Gods and Thoth the Baboon shone in the night sky. This was the mercy of Ra to the children of his tears.

Lastly, Ra ordered Nun and Geb to guard the earth from the chaos serpents and he made Osiris King of Egypt and Isis Queen. Osiris proved a wise and kindly ruler who showed the people of Egypt how to grow crops, gave them laws and taught them to know and worship the gods. He even made a long journey through the other countries of the earth to bring them the same gifts. Seth was jealous and would have liked to seize the throne of Egypt while his brother was away, but Isis had stayed behind to rule the kingdom. She had never trusted Seth and she watched him like a mongoose eyeing a deadly snake.

When Osiris returned safely to Egypt there was great rejoicing and even Seth pretended to be pleased. He had already begun to plot against his brother and had found a group of greedy, discontented men to help him. Seth waited patiently until his chance came and at last he was invited to a banquet at his brother's palace on a night when he knew that Isis would be away.

Generous Osiris loved to give splendid banquets to the whole court so Seth's fellow conspirators were there among the guests. As soon as the king's brother arrived he began to talk about a splendid chest that had just been made for him. When the wine had been passed round several times, Seth sent for the chest and all the guests admired the fine wood and the rich gilding. Laughingly, Seth promised to give the chest to any man who could fit it exactly.

The guests crowded round, eager to try their luck, but when they tried to lie down inside the chest some were too short to fit it and others far too tall. Seth knew that only one man there could fit the chest exactly for he had already bribed one of Osiris' servants to find out the king's measurements. When all the other guests had failed, the conspirators gathered round Osiris, pressing him to try.

Trustingly, Osiris allowed himself to be helped into the chest. He lay back and everyone saw that the king fitted comfortably, with his head and heels just touching the ends of the chest. There was laughter among the innocent guests to think that Seth had lost such a prize to his brother. Osiris himself smiled up at Seth and began to speak but his brother signalled to the conspirators. Suddenly the lid of the chest was slammed down and the bolts driven home. While the conspirators held back the innocent guests, Seth sealed the chest with molten lead and Osiris died.

The chest that had become a coffin was carried through the night to the bank of one of the Nile's many branches where the conspirators threw it into the water, hoping that it would drift out to sea and be lost for ever. Then Seth announced the sudden death of his brother and crowned himself as the new king.

When Isis heard the terrible news she was half mad with grief. She cut off a lock of her hair and dressed in the sombre clothes of a widow. Then she set out to look for her husband's body. Wild

rumours were everywhere but for a long time she could learn nothing definite. Isis trudged from village to village, questioning everyone she met and at last she spoke to some children who had actually seen the chest thrown into the Nile and float downstream.

The goddess followed that branch of the Nile until it joined the sea. Every few days she found someone who had glimpsed a gilded chest floating north and she knew that all she could do was follow. Isis left Egypt and wandered along the coastline through strange countries until she came to the kingdom of Byblos. There the people could talk of little but a miraculous tree that had suddenly sprung up on the seashore.

The coffin of Osiris had drifted ashore and into the roots of a sapling. Strengthened by the murdered god, the sapling grew in a single night into a tall and graceful tree. When the King of Byblos heard about this marvel he sent his carpenters to chop down the tree and bring it to his palace to be used as a pillar. The carpenters obeyed and trimmed the felled trunk to make a fine pillar; no-one suspected that the coffin of a god was hidden inside the tree.

When Isis learned about the tree from villagers eager to gossip with a stranger, she made her way into the city of Byblos and sat down by a fountain close to the palace.

When some of the maids of the Queen of Byblos came out to the fountain to draw water, they noticed Isis and asked her who she was. The goddess simply told them that she was an Egyptian and a skilled hairdresser. Then and there Isis cunningly plaited the maids' hair and breathed on their skin so that a divine fragrance clung to them.

As soon as the girls went back into the palace

everyone began to admire their attractive hairstyles and marvellous perfume. The maids told their mistress, Queen Athenais, about the Egyptian woman at the fountain and Isis was sent for. The goddess plaited the Queen's hair and Athenais was so delighted that she asked Isis to stay in the palace. In a short while Queen Athenais came to like and trust the Egyptian stranger and Isis was made nurse to the youngest of the two princes of Byblos.

Every night when the rest of the palace was asleep, Isis crept into the room with the pillar that held her husband's coffin and wept over him. In the daytime she looked after the baby prince.

Isis grew fond of the baby and decided to make him immortal. One night she took him with her to the room where the pillar stood and kindled a fire. She whispered spells over it and laid the sleeping baby in the flames. The fire began to burn away the little prince's humanity but Isis did not watch over him. She turned herself into a swallow and flew round and round the pillar, lamenting her murdered husband with the high, sad voice of a bird.

Queen Athenais, who slept in a nearby room, was woken by the crackling of flames and got up to trace the noise. She opened the door to the pillar room and screamed in horror as she saw her child burning. At once the swallow turned back into a woman and the magic flames died away. Isis told the terrified queen who she was and warned her that the little prince would never now be immortal.

Athenais wept at her mistake and asked how she could serve the goddess. Isis asked for the pillar and took it out from under the roof as easily as plucking a lotus. The goddess cut away the trunk, poured oil on the timbers and wrapped them in linen before giving them to Queen Athenais to be kept and honoured in the temple of Byblos.

Isis was given the best boat in the harbour and a crew to sail it and the coffin was carried aboard. When they reached the Egyptian coast, Isis had the coffin taken ashore in a desolate place. Then she unsealed the lid. The body of Osiris looked as if he was merely asleep and the goddess Isis embraced it lovingly,

sobbing wildly in her uncontrollable grief.

The coffin was closed again and Isis journeyed south through the marshes of Lower Egypt. One night when the goddess was asleep, Seth came hunting in the marshes and found the coffin. He recognized it at once and was afraid. Opening the coffin, the cruel god lifted out his brother's corpse and tore it in pieces. Then he scattered the pieces throughout Egypt, certain that Isis would never find them all.

When Isis discovered the empty coffin her cry of anguish reached to the heavens and Nephthys her sister hurried to help her. Though Nephthys was the wife of Seth, she had always loved Isis and Osiris better so together the two daughters of Nut set out to search for the scattered body.

For long, sad years faithful Isis and gentle Nephthys wandered through Egypt and in every place where they found a fragment of Osiris they set up a shrine. At last all the pieces were gathered together and Isis worked the greatest of her spells to make the body whole again. The two goddesses watched over the body in the form of hawks, shading it with their wings, while Isis prayed that Osiris should be restored.

She tried every spell she knew and managed to revive Osiris for one night of love so that her promised child could be conceived. Then the body of Osiris was truly dead but his spirit lived on. Ra-Atum made Osiris King of the Dead in the realm of the Beautiful West and from that time onwards every Egyptian knew that death was nothing to fear, for his spirit would live on in the Kingdom of Osiris.

Horus, the falcon-headed son of Isis and Osiris, was born in the marshes of Chemmis and many stories are told of his perilous childhood there. About two and a half thousand years ago, one of these stories was inscribed on a statue of Horus which shows him strangling snakes and scorpions and trampling on crocodiles. The Egyptians believed that if someone who had been bitten by a snake or a scorpion drank water that had been poured over this statue he might be healed, as Horus once was, by the power of the gods.

The inscription tells how Isis and her baby son were caught by Seth outside the marshes. Pretending that it was all for her own protection,

Seth shut Isis up in a spinning house and forced her to spin flax all day. The goddess was closely guarded and without help she was afraid to try to escape with so young a baby.

It was not long, however, before Thoth discovered where Isis was hidden. The wise god entered the spinning house, unseen by the guards, and spoke to Isis.

'You must leave here quickly and return to the sacred marshes of Chemmis where Seth cannot follow you. Wait there till Horus is old enough to claim his father's throne and then we shall see justice done!'

Thoth told Isis how to plan her escape and left behind him seven magic scorpions who would be her guards on the journey north. That night Isis slipped out of the spinning house with Horus in her arms and the scorpions scuttling in front.

By the time she had walked all night and most of the next day carrying her sleeping child, Isis was exhausted and longed for somewhere to rest. At last she and her scorpions came to a village and Isis paused outside the largest house, hoping to be invited in. When the rich woman who owned the house saw the scorpions she was frightened and slammed the door on the weary mother and child. Isis prepared to trudge on but a poor fisherman's daughter opened the door of

her tiny hut and asked the travellers to share what little she had.

While Isis rested in the poor girl's hut and shared her supper of coarse bread and dried fish, the scorpions muttered together against the rich woman. The magical creatures pooled all their poison in the sting of their leader, Tefen, and the scorpion crawled under the gates of the rich woman's house.

Beside an open window the rich woman's only son was sleeping next to his nurse. Tefen crept onto the bed and stung the child. He woke with a scream and the nurse was roused quickly enough to see a huge scorpion scuttling away. She shouted for her mistress and the whole house was soon in as much uproar as if there had been a fire or a flood. The rich woman snatched up her child and ran from house to house but her neighbours were too afraid now to help her.

When Isis heard what had happened, she looked down at Horus sleeping contentedly in her arms and felt sorry for the rich woman. 'An innocent child shall not die because of me,' said the goddess and she called to the rich woman to bring her the child.

Trembling with fear, the woman carried her son into the poor girl's hut. His skin was already burning with fever and he was panting for breath. Isis stood up and laid her hands on the boy, ordering the poison of Tefen to leave him: 'I am Isis, the Mistress of Magic. Every poisonous creature obeys me. Let the child live and the poison die. Let Horus be well for his mother Isis and let this child be well for his mother!'

At once the fever died away; the child's skin was cool again and he was breathing normally. Now that the rich woman knew who it was that she had turned from her door she was more upset than ever. She took her son away and put him to bed and then carried her richest possessions to the hut of the fisherman's daughter, in the hope of pleasing the goddess.

Isis was glad to see the poor girl rewarded for her kindness and in the morning the goddess and her son continued their journey. They soon reached the marshes of Chemmis in safety and the young god was hidden among the papyrus thickets and lotus pools. Whenever she left the marshes to fetch food, Isis disguised herself as a beggar woman but she did not always leave a guard with Horus. She never imagined that any danger could come to the young god as he played in the mud beside the still waters.

One day when Isis returned to the marshes Horus did not toddle forward as usual to greet her. The golden child was lying on his back in the mud, with water streaming from his eyes and mouth. His body was limp and when Isis laid her head to his chest the heartbeat was very faint.

The goddess chanted spells but as she did not know the name of her son's sickness, she could not drive it out. As her magic failed her, Isis began to cry. Who could she turn to? Her husband was dead, her brother was a deadly enemy and her sister was powerless to help her. The gods were remote, but men were close, in a fishing village on the edge of the marshes. Isis ran there with Horus in her arms.

At her cries of distress the fishermen came out of their huts and they pitied her as they would pity any mother with a sick child. The fishermen tried the simple remedies they knew but Horus only grew weaker. Then one of them fetched a wise woman who was staying in the village. She came to Isis carrying a powerful amulet, the Sign of Life, and took Horus in her arms.
'Don't be afraid, little Horus,' murmured the wise woman. 'Mother of the god, do not despair. Horus is protected from his uncle's malice in the marshes of Chemmis. Seth dare not enter them, but he must have sent a snake or a scorpion to bite and poison Horus.'

Then Isis leaned down to smell the child's breath and knew that the wise woman was right: Horus had been poisoned.

Horus began to moan with pain while the villagers looked on helplessly. Suddenly Nephthys appeared. She had sensed her sister's grief and hastened to Chemmis; with her was Selkis, the scorpion goddess. While Nephthys wept in sympathy, Selkis examined the child. She soon saw that there was nothing she could do for him, the fever was raging through his small body and he would soon be dead.
'Isis, you must cry out to the heavens,' said Selkis. 'Stop the Sun Boat! Then the cosmic wind will cease to blow and time will end, unless

Horus is healed. Hurry, or it will be too late.'

Isis looked up to where the gods rowed Ra across the skies in the Boat of Millions of Years and she gave a terrible cry. The whole earth shuddered and the sun stopped, for Isis had power over Ra because she knew his secret name.

When the King of the Gods found that his boat could not move he sent Thoth down to Egypt to find out what had happened.
'What is the matter, Isis?' asked Thoth. 'Surely nothing can have happened to Horus? Why have you stopped the Sun Boat and brought darkness to lands which should be in light?'
'Horus is poisoned,' said Isis bitterly, 'and Seth is to blame. I wish now that I had died with Osiris, I only stayed behind to see Horus avenge his father.'
'Don't be afraid Isis, don't cry Nephthys, I have come from the sky with the breath of life to cure your child.'

Then the wise god began to chant a spell:
'Back, O poison! You are to be vanquished by the power of Ra himself. The King of the Gods commands you to go from this child. The Sun Boat will stand still and half of the world will wither and burn and half will lie in darkness, until Horus is healed. Down to the earth, O poison, so that the sun may journey across the sky again and all hearts rejoice.'

Then the poison began to leave Horus and Thoth sang out, 'The fever is gone, the poison is vanquished! Horus is healed—to his mother's delight!'

Isis said quickly, 'Order the marsh-dwellers to protect Horus.' Thoth agreed and ordered the people and creatures of the marshes to watch over the child until he was old enough to claim his father's throne.
'Ra himself will guard Horus,' promised the wise god, 'and the power of his mother will protect him for she will make everyone love him. I must return to the Sun Boat for they cannot row on without me. I must take the good news to Ra that Horus is alive and well—to his mother's delight.'

Then Thoth returned to the sky and Isis joyfully carried her son back into the marshes, to wait for the time of her vengeance on Seth.

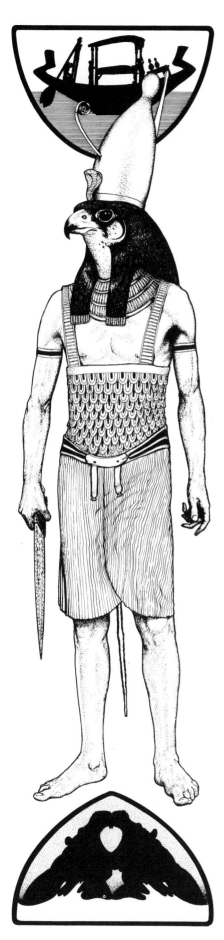

The conflict of Horus and Seth

As soon as Horus was old enough to challenge his uncle Seth he summoned the Ennead, and many of the other gods, to act as judges. With his mother beside him, Horus spoke of the cruel murder of his father Osiris and of how Seth had usurped the throne of Egypt. All the gods were impressed by the eloquence of falcon-headed Horus and when they had listened to the whole of his story they also pitied him.

Shu, the eldest son of the Creator spoke first: 'Right should rule might. Seth had force on his side but Horus has justice. We should do Horus justice by saying "Yes, you shall have the throne of your father." '

Then Thoth said to the Ennead, 'This is right a million times!'

Isis gave a great cry of joy and begged the north wind to change direction and blow westward to whisper the news to Osiris. 'Giving the throne to Horus seems right to the whole Ennead!' declared Shu.

All this time no-one had thought to ask the King of the Gods what he thought about the case.

'What's this?' muttered Ra-Atum. 'Are the Ennead starting to make decisions on their own?'

Shu did not notice that his father's face had darkened and he went on confidently, 'Thoth shall give the royal signet ring to Horus and we will crown him with the White Crown.'

All the gods shouted their approval; all but two. The Sun God was ominously silent and Seth himself suddenly stepped forward and bellowed, 'If there is any dispute about who should rule Egypt, let this puny boy challenge me in person. Then all you gods can watch me overthrow him!'

'We know that would be wrong,' protested Thoth. 'How can we give the throne of Osiris to you when the son of Osiris stands before us? He is the rightful heir, we are all agreed on that.'

'I have not agreed,' said the Sun God coldly.

There was a shocked silence and then Shu wailed, 'What shall we do now?'

The best they could think of was to send for the ancient ram god of Mendes and to ask him to judge between Horus and Seth. So

Banebdjed was hastily sent for and when the ancient god arrived, Ra-Atum said to him, 'Come now, judge between these two young gods, so that they'll stop their wrangling over Egypt and give us some peace.'

Banebdjed knew that Horus was in the right but he was afraid of angering the Sun God so he said, 'We should not decide the matter without the very best advice. Let us send a letter to Neith, the Divine Mother. Let us see what she thinks about it.'

Then the Ennead said to Thoth, 'Write her a letter at once!'
'I will, I will,' promised the scribe of the gods. He blackened the tip of his reed brush, unrolled a piece of papyrus and squatted down to write a flowery letter to Neith. The swiftest of messengers was sent north to deliver the Ennead's letter to the great goddess. Neith read it and soon sent back a letter of her own.

Thoth unrolled the papyrus and read the letter aloud. 'Give the throne of Osiris to Horus his son. To do anything else would be so wicked that the sky would crash down on your heads. As for Seth, double his goods, give him two beautiful goddesses to be his wives and let him leave the throne to Horus.'

Then all the gods shouted, 'This goddess is right!'

The Sun God was very angry and he said contemptuously to Horus, 'How can a feeble boy like you rule Egypt?'

The other gods were angry then and the baboon god Baba stood up and said to Ra-Atum, 'Your shrine is empty; we aren't taking any notice of you!'

The Sun God was so shocked and offended that he covered his face and lay down on his back. The Ennead realized that they had gone too far and shouted at Baba, 'Leave this company at once!' They tried to comfort Ra-Atum but he refused to listen to them. He got up, stalked into his tent and would not come out again.

Nobody could think what to do next and they were all afraid of what might happen to the world if Ra-Atum refused to sail the Sun Boat across the skies. Finally Hathor, the daughter of Ra-Atum, decided on a plan. The beautiful goddess began to dance and as she danced she stripped off all her clothes. The other gods crowded round to get a better view, laughing and applauding. The noise disturbed the Sun God and he thrust his head through his tent flap to find out what was going on. When he saw his lovely daughter dancing, Ra-Atum laughed too and forgot his anger. The King of the Gods returned to sit with the Ennead and said to Horus and Seth, 'We will hear the case again and both of you can put your point of view.'

Seth insisted on speaking first. 'I am Seth, the strongest of the Ennead. When the Sun Boat voyages through the undersky and the serpents of chaos attack, only I can save you. I am the protector of the gods so you should give the throne of Osiris to me!'

Remembering the terrors of the chaos serpents, many of the gods muttered that Seth was right but Shu and Thoth still said, 'How can we give the throne to the uncle when the son and heir is standing here?'

Banebdjed answered, 'How can we give the throne to a youngster when his elder is standing here?'

Then Horus said bitterly, 'Will you rob me of my birthright in front of the Ennead?'

Isis was furious with the Ennead for not speaking up for her son and she complained to them until for the sake of peace they promised that justice should be done to Horus. Then it was Seth's turn to be angry.
'How dare you cowards go back on your word? I shall fetch my great sceptre and strike one of you down with it each day and I swear that I won't argue my case in any court where Isis is present!'

To keep the peace Ra-Atum said, 'We shall cross the river to the Island-in-the Midst and try the case there. I will give orders to Nemty the ferryman not to ferry Isis across, or any woman that might be her.' Then the Ennead and all the other gods and goddesses crossed the river and set up their splendid tents on the island.

Cunning Isis, the Mistress of Magic, changed herself into a bent old woman carrying a jar of flour and honey cakes. She hobbled towards the riverbank where Nemty the ferryman was sitting beside his boat. 'Now young man,' croaked Isis,

'ferry me across at once. In this pot I have food for the young man who is tending cattle on the island. He's been with the herd five days now and his food will have run out.'
'I'm sorry, grandmother,' said Nemty, 'but I have orders not to ferry women across this river.'

Isis delved into her pot. 'I will give you this sweet cake for payment.'

Nemty did not even glance at it. 'I am the ferryman of the gods, what do I need with your cakes?'

Then Isis thrust a skinny finger in front of Nemty's face. 'Do you see this gold ring on my finger? Ferry me across and it's yours.'

The ring was a very fine one and Nemty could not resist such a bribe. 'Alright then, grandmother, give me that ring and I'll ferry you over.' He picked up his pole and they were soon across.
'Hurry back when you've found your cowherd,' shouted Nemty as he tied up his boat.

Isis was already slipping through the trees towards the camp of the Ennead. The gods were holding a feast but Seth was standing apart from the cheerful company. Changing her shape again, Isis walked towards Seth as a beautiful woman, dressed like a widow. Her brother might be the strongest of the gods but she knew that she could always defeat him by cunning. Isis smiled and Seth hurried to greet this attractive stranger, eager to please her.

'Who are you, my pretty?' asked Seth. 'And why have you come here?'

Isis hid her face and pretended to cry. 'O great Lord, I am looking for a champion. I was the happy wife of a herdsman and I gave him a son. Then my dear husband died and the boy began to look after his father's cattle. One day a strange man came and siezed our byre and told my son that he was going to take our cattle and turn us out. My son wanted to protest but the man threatened to beat him. Great Lord, help me and be my son's champion.'

Seth put his arms around her. 'Don't cry my pretty. I'll be your champion and thrash this villain. How dare a stranger take the father's property when the son is still alive!'

Then Isis shrieked with laughter. She turned herself into a kite and flew up into an acacia tree. 'Cry yourself, mighty Seth. You have condemned yourself! You have judged your own case.'

Seth was so angry he wept tears of rage and the other gods demanded to know what had upset him.
'That evil woman has tricked me again,' complained Seth and he told them what had happened.

Then the Sun God said, 'It is true Seth, you have judged yourself, now what will you do?'
'First, I will see that ferryman punished!' growled Seth.

Nemty was brought before the gods and as a

45

punishment for disobeying orders, they cut off his toes. From that day on Nemty never looked at gold again.

Now the Ennead crossed over the river and camped in the Western Mountains while plans were made for the coronation of Horus. Seth still would not admit defeat. He watched the White Crown placed on the feathered head of Horus and said fiercely, 'He may be crowned but he can't rule until he's beaten me. I challenge you Horus; let us turn ourselves into hippopotami and fight deep in the river. Whoever surfaces first will be the loser!' Horus agreed gladly but Isis sat down and wept, afraid that Seth would kill her son.

The two gods were soon transformed into huge, fierce hippopotami and they plunged into the river. Isis quickly took yarn and copper and made them into a magical harpoon. She threw the weapon into the white water churned up by the fighting beasts, but she could not tell which god was which. The copper point stabbed Horus in the flank and he surfaced briefly and roared, 'Mother your spear has pierced me, let me go!'

Isis called to her magic weapon to release Horus and it returned to her hand. She threw it again and this time it stabbed Seth. With a bellow of pain Seth rose up as Isis tugged at the harpoon and cried out, 'O my sister, why must you always be my enemy? What have I done to you? I am your brother, let me go!'

As Isis could not help feeling a little sorry for Seth, she ordered her magic weapon to release him. Horus was furious with his mother for interfering and for pitying Seth. He leaped out of the river with a face like a leopard and cut off his mother's head with one stroke from his copper knife. Then Horus strode towards the Mountains of the West, carrying his mother's head under his arm.

Isis, the Mistress of Magic, calmly turned her body into a statue and walked towards the tent of the Sun God. All the gods and goddesses jumped up in amazement and Ra-Atum said to Thoth, 'Who is this coming with no head?'
'It is Isis,' answered the wisest of the gods, 'and Horus has cut off her head.'

The Sun God was horrified and vowed that Horus should be punished. Isis was soon restored to her usual form and the Ennead went up into the Western Mountains to look for Horus.

The young god had found an oasis and was asleep in the shadow of a palm tree when his uncle discovered him. Seth seized Horus from behind and tore out both his eyes. The young god cried out in terrible agony as Seth strode away and buried the eyes of Horus in the ground. When he returned to the camp of the Ennead, Seth told them that he had found no trace of his nephew.

All through the night poor blind Horus lay in pain and by the morning two beautiful lotuses had grown up where his eyes were buried. Hathor, Lady of the Southern Sycamore, had continued to search for Horus long after the other gods had given up and at last she found him and pitied his agony. Hathor the great huntress caught a gazelle and milked it. Then she knelt beside the young god and said gently, 'Uncover your face.'

Horus did as he was told and Hathor dripped the milk onto his wounds. At once the pain vanished.
'Open your eyes,' commanded Hathor. Horus obeyed and found that the healing magic of the goddess had restored his eyes and he could see again. Hathor hurried back to the Ennead and said, 'Seth has been lying to you. He found Horus yesterday and tore out his eyes, but I have healed him and here he comes!'

Then the Ennead ordered Horus and Seth to stand before the Sun God and hear his judgement. Since both of them had acted wrongly Ra-Atum said, 'For the last time, stop quarrelling and make peace!' Seth pretended to agree and as a gesture of good will even asked Horus to stay with him in his palace. Horus, however, soon found that he could not trust his uncle and he had to ask his mother for help again. Isis willingly forgave her son and whatever trick Seth tried, she managed to turn it against him.

At last, in desperation, Seth demanded one more contest with Horus. Before the whole Ennead he declared, 'Let both of us build a ship of stone and we'll race them down the Nile. Whoever wins the race shall wear the crown of

to stop and he had to obey the great gods.

By this time, Horus despaired of his case ever being settled so he journeyed north to seek the advice of the wise goddess Neith. In the meantime Shu and Thoth persuaded the Ennead to send a letter to Osiris himself in the Beautiful West, the realm of the dead. The journey to that realm was long and perilous but at last a messenger arrived with an angry letter from the King of the Dead. Osiris demanded to know why his son had been robbed of the throne and whether the gods had forgotten that it was Osiris who had given the world the precious gifts of barley and wheat.

When Thoth read this letter aloud to the Ennead the Sun God was annoyed at Osiris for telling him what to do and he wrote back an arrogant letter. After many days another weary messenger returned with a second letter from the King of the Dead and Thoth read it out: 'How good are the deeds of the Ennead!' began Osiris sarcastically. 'Justice has sunk into the underworld. Now listen to me, the land of the dead is full of demons who fear no god or goddess. If I send them out into the world of the living they will bring back the hearts of evildoers to the place of punishment. Who among you is more powerful than I? Even the gods must come at last to the Beautiful West.'

When the Sun God heard this letter, even he was afraid and all the gods agreed that the wish of Osiris should be honoured. Isis herself was sent to bind Seth and bring him in chains before the Ennead.
'Seth, have you stolen the throne from Horus?' demanded the Sun God.

Seth said meekly, 'No, let Horus be brought and given his father's throne.'

The young god was crowned again and placed on the throne of Egypt and Isis gave a joyful shout: 'My son you are King; my heart is glad that the whole earth will be brightened with your glory!'

Then the Sun God had Seth released from his chains and said to him, 'Son of Nut, you shall live with me in the sky as the Lord of Storms and when you thunder the whole earth will tremble!'

Seth was satisfied at last and made his peace with Horus and all the gods rejoiced.

Osiris.' Horus agreed to the contest at once.

Mighty Seth took up his club and struck the top of a nearby mountain. Then he built a huge ship of solid stone and dragged it to the river. Horus' ship was already afloat, for the young god had secretly made a boat of pine and plastered it to make it look like stone. When Seth tried to launch his boat it sank straight to the bottom of the Nile and the Ennead laughed. Seth leaped into the water and turned himself into a hippopotamus once more. He attacked the boat of Horus and because it was only wood it splintered and sank. Horus grabbed his spear and thrust at Seth but the Ennead shouted at him

The journey of the soul

Each dawn Ra the Sun God, in his scarab beetle form, boarded the 'Day Boat' and was rowed across the sky by a crew of gods and the souls of the blessed dead. At noon the youthful sun was strong and blazed down on the earth, but by dusk he had changed into ancient ram-headed Atum. When he reached the western horizon, Ra-Atum boarded the 'Night Boat' and travelled across the sky below the earth and the realm of the dead. Thoth, Hathor, Seth and many other deities surrounded and protected Ra-Atum and the boat of the Night Sun was dragged by jackals and crowned cobras. The dead woke into new life as the Sun God lit up the underworld and Osiris, the ruler of the Beautiful West, saluted Ra-Atum as his twin soul, for they were both images of the Creator.

The Night Sun had to overcome many obstacles on his perilous journey. The terrible demons who guarded the gates of the underworld would not open them unless their mysterious questions were correctly answered and the forces of chaos gathered nightly to attack Ra-Atum. Mighty Seth stood in the prow to fight off Apophis, the greatest of the chaos serpents, for if the sun did not win free of the underworld the waters of chaos would cover the earth and the rule of the gods would end. Every dawn was a hard fought victory of light over darkness, order over chaos.

When an Egyptian king died he was thought to share the ordeal of the Night Sun and his journey through the dangers of the underworld led to a dawn of rebirth and eternal life. The dead king was also identified with Osiris who had suffered death, risen again to rule the underworld and had been avenged by Horus. Every king followed the same pattern of death and rebirth, while his son replaced him on the throne of Egypt as the new Horus.

These ideas, and many others about the afterlife of the king, occur in the spells carved inside some pyramids. At first such spells were only used in royal burials but after the collapse of the Old Kingdom, important commoners began to have the spells painted on their coffins, together with maps of the underworld. By the New Kingdom every dead Egyptian was identified with Osiris and the spells were written on papyrus and buried with the dead. These spells made a book of some one hundred and ninety chapters which the

Egyptians called 'The Spells for Coming Forth by Day' but which is better known now as 'The Book of the Dead'.

All Egyptians went to a great deal of trouble and expense to prepare their tombs and burial equipment. A fine coffin or an illustrated copy of the Book of the Dead were status symbols which showed how wealthy and successful the owner was. The bodies of the dead went through the elaborate and costly process of mummification. In very early times the Egyptians had simply buried their dead wrapped in mats in shallow graves in the desert. The hot, dry sand had preserved the bodies but when the dead began to be buried in wooden coffins inside mudbrick or rock-cut tombs, the bodies decayed. The Egyptians noticed this and tried to develop a method of imitating the effect of the hot sand so that bodies could be preserved and the spirits of the dead could still inhabit them. This art of mummification reached its peak just after the end of the New Kingdom.

When someone died, the grieving relatives would take the body to the embalmers, who lived as a caste apart and wore the jackal mask of their patron, Anubis, the guardian of the dead. When a price for their services had been agreed, the body was laid on a stone slab and the embalmers began their grisly work. A metal hook was used to pull out the brains through the nostrils. The brains were then thrown away since the Egyptians did not recognize their importance and thought of the heart as the centre of intelligence and feeling. Next the stomach was slit open and the vital organs were removed. The inside of the body was rinsed out with wine and packed with herbs and spices. Then the whole body was covered in natron for at least forty days.

Natron is a natural mixture of carbonate, bicarbonate, chloride and sulphate of sodium which absorbs water. The vital organs were also treated with natron and the lungs, liver, stomach and intestines were then packed into four 'Canopic' jars, stone jars with stoppers in the form of the four sons of Horus. After forty days the body itself was completely dry and little but skin and bone remained. The embalmers used bags of myrrh and cinnamon, or humbler

materials such as sand or sawdust to stuff the body, plumping out the limbs and face and making them look more life-like. The heart was replaced in the chest and the stomach was sewn up again. The body was anointed with scented oils and sometimes treated with molten resin before being carefully bandaged with strips of linen. Numerous amulets were hidden in the layers of bandaging and a mask was placed over the head of the completed mummy.

The body was then laid inside a set of painted coffins and taken across the Nile to one of the Cities of the Dead on the West Bank. Loaded onto a sledge, it would be dragged by oxen to the family tomb with the relatives walking behind and professional mourners beating their breasts, tearing their hair and wailing for the dead man as if he was Osiris himself. At the entrance to the tomb a priest performed the 'Opening of the Mouth' ceremony in which he touched the mask of the mummy with a model adze and recited spells to restore the power of sight and speech and hearing to the dead.

The mummy could then be inhabited by the dead man's *ka*. The *ka* appeared as the double of his earthly body but it was the vital force which survived him after death. The *ka* could live in the dead man's mummy or, if that had been destroyed, in a statue of him, but it needed constant nourishment. Every Egyptian was supposed to make food offerings at the tombs of his ancestors but the duty was often neglected or forgotten. Knowing this the Egyptians included pictures of models of food and drink and all the other good things in life in their tombs for the use of the dead. As an extra precaution some tombs were inscribed with a message from the dead promising to reward anyone who would recite a spell to invoke 'bread, beer, oxen, fowl, alabaster, clothing and all good and pure things on which a god lives.'

Though the Egyptians sometimes adopted new ideas, they hardly ever discarded old ones. Because of this their beliefs about death and the afterlife can seen very complicated or plain contradictory. The tomb was the 'house of the *ka*' and the scenes of daily life carved or painted on the walls and the clothes and jewels and furniture buried with the dead make it look as if the Egyptians imagined the afterlife taking place in the tomb and being very like life in Egypt. This is partly true, but it is not the whole story.

As well as a *ka* every Egyptian was thought to have a *ba* or soul, which was shown as a bird with a human head. After death a man or woman's *ba* could take on the form of a swallow or a falcon or a heron and fly wherever it liked on earth with flocks of other souls. Nor was the *ba* confined to earth; it also made a perilous journey through the underworld to win the right to an afterlife of eternal joy.

Most of the spells in the Book of the Dead were designed to help the *ba* as it shared many of the dangers faced by the Night Sun on its voyage. All kinds of terrible things might happen to the *ba* in the underworld and spells were needed to stop him losing his heart, being bitten by snakes, forced to walk upside-down or decapitated.

The *ba* had to endure ordeals of fire and water and might be attacked by monsters such as the Ass-Eating Serpent or the Crocodiles of the Four Quarters, which could only be defeated by using the right spell against them. Before he could get across the Lake of Dawn to the Winding Water, the *ba* had to name the surly ferryman of the gods and every part of his magic boat. Finally he had to face a series of gates guarded by hideous demons who threatened him with their knives. By knowing the secret names of these demons—Faceless One, Wallower in Slime, Clawed One, Feeder on Carrion and Lord of Knives—the *ba* gained power over them.

His goal was the throne room of Osiris, the Hall of the Two Truths, but the *ba* could not enter without speaking the names of every part of the doorway.

Inside the Hall of the Two Truths, the *ba* was met by Thoth and taken to face the forty-two judges of the underworld. He had to greet them by name and swear that he had not committed the crimes that they punished.
'O Long-Strider who comes from Heliopolis; I have done no evil; Flame-Embracer who comes from Kheraha, I have not robbed; O Long-Nosed One who comes from Hermopolis, I have not been envious; Shadow-Eater who comes from the Twin Caverns, I have not been

dishonest; O Savage-Faced One who comes from Rostau, I have not murdered . . . O you gods, I know your names and I am not afraid! I have lived in truth and done what gods and men admired. I have given bread to the hungry, water to the thirsty, clothes to the naked and ferried the boatless. I have made offerings to the gods and to the dead, I am pure of mouth and hands!'

To test the innocence of the *ba*, his heart was weighed by Anubis against the feather that symbolized *Maat*, while Thoth stood by to record the verdict. The Egyptians were so afraid of this test that they took to burying a Heart Scarab with most mummies. This was a stone scarab beetle inscribed with a spell to help them in the Hall of the Two Truths: 'O heart of my being, don't witness against me, don't oppose me in the place of judgement, don't rebel against me before the guardian of the scales, don't make my name stink before the judges!'

If the heart was weighed down by the sins and heavier than *Maat*, the *ba* died a second and more terrible death. If the scales were even the victorious *ba* was led by Horus before the throne of Osiris and became an *akh*, a blessed soul. The *akh* might shine among the circumpolar stars or join the crew of the Sun Boat or live in bliss in the peaceful Field of Reeds.

Not every Egyptian believed in a happy afterlife or that spells and offerings and mummification could really help the dead. Some poets pointed to the plundered tombs and empty coffins of long dead kings and nobles and urged their listeners: 'Follow your heart as long as you live! Put myrrh on your head, dress in fine linen and rub yourself with oils fit for a god. Heap up your joys and don't let your heart sink. Wailing saves nobody from the grave. Make holiday, make holiday, never weary of it. No-one can take his goods with him; the dead do not return.'

Others trusted in the goodness of the gods and the promised joys of the land of eternity, 'The right and just which holds no terrors. All our ancestors rest in it from the beginning of time. Those yet to be born, millions upon millions, will all come to it, for no-one can linger in the land of Egypt. Our time on earth is only like a dream and God says "Welcome in peace" to those who reach the Beautiful West.'

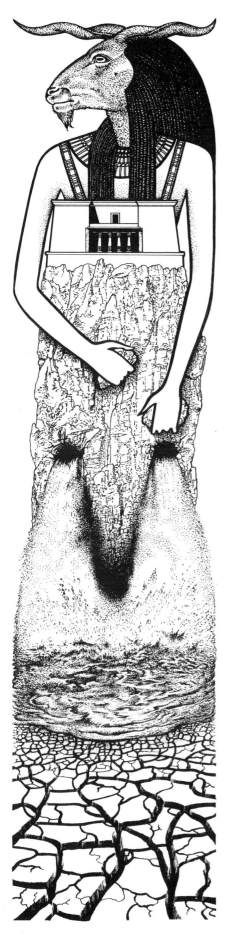

The seven year famine

On an island in the Nile, close to the ancient city of Elephantine, stands a granite rock carved with a story and a scene of a king with three deities: Khnum, Satis and Anukis. The picture and the inscription are about two thousand years old, but the story is set in the reign of King Zoser who ruled Egypt over four and a half thousand years ago.

The story shows how vital the river Nile was to the people of ancient Egypt. The Blue Nile rises in the mountains of Ethiopia and the White Nile in the lakes and marshes of central Africa. The two rivers join near Khartoum, the capital of the Sudan, and flow on towards Egypt. Each year heavy summer rains in Ethiopia and the Sudan swell the Nile. Nowadays the river is controlled by the great Aswan Dam but in ancient times the swollen Nile poured into Egypt and flooded the low-lying land. This inundation covered the Nile valley with a layer of rich mud which was ideal for growing crops when the waters sank low enough for planting to begin. A powerful flood might reach the settlements on the higher ground and do a great deal of damage, but a weak flood, a 'low Nile' was worse. If the flood waters failed to spread out very far, Egypt faced starvation.

In the eighteenth year of Zoser's reign, the Nile failed to rise and flood the land with its life-giving waters. For six years Egypt had suffered low Niles. The floods had only reached half the fields and not enough crops could be grown to feed everyone. Every year the people had prayed for a high Nile and every year the waters had sunk lower. By the seventh year Zoser was in despair.

All kinds of food were scarce. Men robbed their brothers to get enough to eat; children wailed with hunger in their mother's arms; old men squatted in the dust hugging their knees and even the nobles were gaunt and grim. The temples were shut for lack of offerings and the shrines of the gods were deserted.

None of the king's advisers knew what to do until Zoser consulted his vizier, the wise Imhotep.
'Tell me,' said Zoser, 'where is the source of the Nile? Where is the city of the Sinuous One? What god lives there? If I knew that, I could pray to him for help in ending our seven years of famine.'

Imhotep was famous for his skill in architecture and medicine and every other branch of learning, but even he could not answer the king's questions straight away. 'Sovereign, my lord,' said Imhotep, 'I shall go to the temple of Thoth and read his sacred books in the House of Life. If the answers exist, I will find them there.'

Imhotep spent many days studying the sacred writings that only he was wise enough to read. He discovered everything that the king wanted to know and hurried back to court to tell him. 'Sovereign, my lord, far to the south, on an island in the Nile lies the city of Elephantine. It is built on that first mound of land that rose from the dark waters of Nun. The hills that surround the city are of red and black granite and are rich in copper and silver and gold, turquoise, carnelian, emerald and jasper. In the heart of the city stands a temple called 'Joy of Life'. Beneath the temple are two caverns where the Nile sleeps until it is time for the river to rise up and bound towards Egypt in a mighty wall of water. 'Khnum is the god who opens the floodgates. He sits enthroned at Elephantine, with his sandals resting on the Nile and his crown touching the sky. Khnum is the lord of barley and wheat, fruit and flowers, birds and fish and animals. All these good things are offered daily in the temple to the great god Khnum, to Anukis his wife, Satis his daughter and the other deities of Elephantine.'

Zoser was delighted to hear of such a wonderful place on the edge of his realm. He hurriedly unrolled the secret books to learn the rituals that would please Khnum and all the gods of Elephantine. Zoser spent the whole day leading processions of priests to make offerings.

That night, as the king slept, he dreamed that ram-headed Khnum stood beside his bed. In his dream, Zoser leaped up and kissed the ground before the god. Khnum spoke kindly to him.

'I am the maker of mankind. My arms are around you all to hold you steady and keep you safe. I have given you precious stones so that the people of Egypt may build temples and adorn the statues of the gods. I am the master of the flood; when I open the two caverns the Nile gushes out to hug your land and kiss your fields. Mourn no longer; now you have called on me, I shall end the seven years of famine. I will make the Nile gush for you and the great flood will shine again on the fertile shores of Egypt.'

Then glorious Khnum faded from the king's sight but when he woke Zoser remembered his dream. He jumped up full of joy and vigour, certain now that Egypt would be saved. In his gratitude for the god's promises, Zoser decreed that Elephantine should belong to Khnum for ever and that one tenth of all the products of Upper Egypt should be offered in his temple. The farmers were to share their harvest, the hunters, fishermen and bird-trappers were to give up part of every catch and the traders were to heap the altars of Khnum with ivory and ebony and all the produce of Africa. The temple 'Joy of Life' was to be kept in perfect repair and its shrines filled with statues in gold and silver and precious stones. The king's commands were carved on granite, so that they should never be forgotten and Khnum kept his promises. For the rest of Zoser's reign and for many years after, High Niles flooded the land.

The Egyptians came to regard the reign of Zoser as the beginning of a golden age. The wise Imhotep was worshipped as a god and Zoser was remembered as the greatest king of the Third Dynasty. The Fourth Dynasty (2575–2465 BC) marked the start of the Old Kingdom in which Egypt was at the height of its splendour.

The country was divided into districts called Nomes and well governed by a series of strong kings and an efficient civil service headed by the vizier. The government made sure that the natural resources of Egypt were fully exploited. When there were High Niles, barley, emmer (a kind of wheat) and flax for spinning into linen were easily grown. The deserts surrounding Egypt proved to be rich in good stone for building and sculpture and turquoise could be fetched from Sinai. Most important of all were the gold mines of the eastern desert and of Nubia. The kings of Egypt soon conquered and occupied Nubia so that they could work the goldmines and open up trade routes to Africa to barter for ivory and ebony, leopard skins and incense. Encouraged by this new wealth, art flourished. Old Kingdom paintings and carvings are full of a confident delight in life that the Egyptians were never to know again.

King Khufu and the magicians

King Khufu came to the throne of Egypt in about 2500 BC and was the builder of the Great Pyramid at Giza. This story describes how Khufu discovered that a new dynasty of kings was soon to rule Egypt.

One day King Khufu felt bored and he challenged his sons to entertain him with stories of magic. Khaefre, the Crown Prince, at once got up to speak:

'I should like to tell your Majesty about a wonder which happened in the time of your forefather, King Nebka. Close to the temple of Ptah lived a lector-priest called Webaoner. He was a favourite of the king and respected throughout Egypt for his wisdom. Everyone admired him except his own wife. She had fallen in love with a handsome young man from Memphis and one day she packed a sandalwood chest with clothes and fine linen and sent it to the young man as a present. He came to Webaoner's house to thank her and it wasn't long before he had agreed to meet her secretly in a pavilion that stood beside a lake in the garden.

'Webaoner's wife ordered the gardener to take food and wine to the pavilion, to spread its floor with comfortable rugs and cushions and to hang scented torches and garlands of flowers from its columns. Everything was done as she had ordered. The young man joined the lector-priest's wife in the pavilion and they spent the day feasting and kissing and plotting how to get rid of Webaoner.

'Soon whenever her husband was away at court she ordered the pavilion to be made ready and spent days and nights there with the young man. The gardener did not dare to disobey his mistress but when he heard drunken laughter coming from the pavilion or saw the young man bathing in the lake, his heart grieved for his master. At last, when gossip began to spread from the household to the town, he resolved to tell Webaoner the truth about his wife. The gardener asked to speak to his master alone and stammered out his story.

'With a face of stone Webaoner opened an ebony chest and took out some wax. He modelled a crocodile the length of his hand and gave it to the gardener. "When you next see that young man bathing in the lake," said the lector-priest, "throw this crocodile after him." The gardener was puzzled but he promised to obey.

'The next day Webaoner was summoned to court. As soon as he had gone, his wife ordered the pavilion to be prepared and sent a message to her lover. Hidden in a clump of reeds, the gardener waited until the young man waded into the lake to bathe and then tossed the wax crocodile after him. As it hit the water it came alive and began to grow and soon the crocodile was seven cubits long. It swam after the young man and before he could scramble ashore it had seized him in its jaws and dragged him under. On a bed of cushions in the pavilion Webaoner's wife waited in vain for her lover to come back.

'After seven days at court the lector-priest said to King Nebka, "Sovereign, my lord, come back with me to my house and I will show you a great marvel." The king agreed to come and he was soon standing on the edge of the lake surrounded by his pages and fan-bearers. The lector-priest spoke a summoning spell and the smooth waters were broken by the most enormous crocodile that the king and his courtiers had ever seen. From this monster's jaws dangled the young man for the spells of Webaoner had kept him alive under the lake.

'The lector-priest ordered the crocodile to open its jaws and it laid the young man on the shore at the king's feet. Nebka backed away. "Indeed this is a fearful crocodile!" Webaoner bent down and as he touched the crocodile it turned back into wax and shrank to the length of his hand. He presented it to the king, told him the whole story and begged for justice.

'King Nebka ordered the young man to be thrown back into the lake and tossed the crocodile after him, saying, "Take what is yours!" It grew again to a monster of seven cubits and seized the wretched lover and dragged him down to his death. As for the wife of Webaoner, King Nebka ordered her to be burned alive. This your majesty was the wonder which happened in the reign of your ancestor Nebka.'

Khufu was very pleased with this story and ordered that offerings of bread and beer, oxen and incense, be made to the spirits of King Nebka and the lector-priest Webaoner. Then Prince Baufre got up to speak:

'I should like to tell your Majesty about a wonder which happened in the reign of your father Sneferu. One hot day King Sneferu wandered from room to room of his palace looking for some new entertainment but found nothing to please or sooth him. Finally he sent for the wise lector-priest Djadja-emankh and asked him to suggest a diversion.

"Let your Majesty take a boat out on the lake in your gardens," began the lector-priest, "and let the rowers be the most beautiful girls in your harem. Then your Majesty's heart will be refreshed by seeing the birds and flowers of the lake and by watching the rowers."

'Sneferu was delighted with this idea. He ordered a boat to be fitted with oars of ebony and gilded sandalwood. "And fetch me twenty young girls with pretty figures and long braided hair. Take away their clothes, dress them in nets and let them row!"

'Everything was done as the king commanded and Sneferu was soon lounging on a couch on the deck of his pleasure-boat while twenty charming girls, dressed only in glittering nets, rowed him round the lake. The king admired the white lotus flowers and the clusters of papyrus that edged the lake, he admired leaping fish and flights of startled birds but most of all he admired the pretty rowers.

'One of the girls rowing at the stroke oar was wearing a fish-shaped turquoise amulet in her braided hair. She was growing so hot as she rowed that she pushed back the braids that fell across her face. Her hand dislodged the turquoise pendant and it fell into the lake and sank. With a squeak of dismay the girl stopped rowing and first the rowers on her side and then those on the other had to stop too.

"What is the matter? Why have you stoppped rowing?" demanded the king.

"I had a new turquoise amulet shaped like a fish," said the girl at the stroke oar. "But now it's fallen in the lake and I've lost it."

"Row on," ordered the king, "and I will soon find you another amulet."

"But I don't want another amulet," said the girl obstinately, "I want my amulet."

'Then Sneferu persuaded the girls to row him to the shore and he sent for Djadja-emankh. "My brother," sighed the king, "I did as you suggested

56

and my heart was glad to see the girls row but now one of them has dropped her turquoise amulet in the lake and she wants it back . . ."

'The wise lector-priest smiled and then murmured a powerful spell. The waters of the lake rolled back towards either bank leaving a dry place in the middle. There, on a potsherd, lay the turquoise amulet. Djadja-emankh went down to the bed of the lake, picked up the amulet and brought it back to its owner. Then he released the waters with a second spell and they surged back to cover the bed of the lake. King Sneferu gave the lector-priest rich rewards and spent the rest of the day in feasting with the pretty rowers. This, your Majesty, was the wonder which happened in the reign of your father King Sneferu.'

Khufu was much amused by this story and he ordered that offerings of bread and beer, oxen and incense, be made to the spirits of King Sneferu and the lector-priest Djadja-emankh. Then Prince Hardjedef, the wisest of Khufu's sons got up to speak:

'Your Majesty, my brothers have told you about wonders in the past but I can tell you of a living wonder, a great magician.'

'Who is this magician, my son, and where does he live?'

'His name is Djedi and he lives in Djed-Sneferu. He is one hundred and ten years old and still eats five hundred loaves every day and drinks a hundred jugs of beer every night. He knows how to join a severed head to its body; he knows how to make a lion follow meekly behind him and he knows the number of the secret chambers in the Temple of Thoth!'

For a long time Khufu had been trying to discover the number and plan of the secret chambers of Thoth so that he could copy them for his own tomb. He said eagerly to Hardjedef, 'Go and fetch this magician at once; take whatever boats you need!' The prince took three boats and sailed south. When the pyramids of Sneferu were seen on the western horizon the boats moored on the banks of the Nile and Hardjedef was carried in a chair of gilded ebony to the village of Djed-Sneferu.

Djedi the magician was lying on a mat outside the door of his house with one servant massaging his head and another washing his feet. The bearers set down the prince's chair and Hardjedef said, 'Greetings, honoured Djedi. Though you are old you have the vigour of youth. I have come to summon you to the court of my father the king where he will entertain you and all your household and reward you with a fine tomb.'

Hardjedef stretched out his hand to help the old man up and together they walked towards the Nile, the magician leaning on the prince's arm. When they reached the river bank Djedi asked for one boat for his family and one for his books of magic. He himself travelled with Hardjedef in the first boat.

The king received them in the pillared throne-room and when Djedi had kissed the ground before him, Khufu said, 'Well, magician, why have I never seen you before?'

'The one who is summoned is the one who comes,' answered Djedi dryly. 'Now that you have summoned me, I am here. What is your command?'

'Is it true,' asked the king, 'that you know how to reattach a severed head?'

'Sovereign, my lord, it is.'

Khufu beckoned the captain of his guard. 'Go to the prison, choose a criminal and bring him here to be beheaded.'

'No,' said Djedi sternly, 'I may not work my spells on men, the cattle of the gods. It is forbidden.'

The king was furious at this contradiction of his orders but the old magician was not afraid of him and stood firm.

'Go to the kitchens then,' growled Khufu, 'and bring us a goose.'

The captain soon returned holding a struggling goose by both wings. He drew a knife, slit its throat and chopped off the head. The goose's body was placed on the west side of the hall and its head on the east side. Djedi stood between them and murmured a spell. The body jerked to its webbed feet and waddled across the hall towards the twitching head. As the two met, the head sprang back onto the goose's neck and began to cackle. There was no trace of a wound.

Khufu could hardly believe what he had just seen and ordered Djedi to try the spell again on a

duck. The old magician murmured the same
spell, the duck's severed head joined its body
and the bird was caught and carried back to the
royal kitchens. Finally Khufu sent for an ox. The
great beast was led into the hall and held by three
men while its head was severed by an axe. Djedi
spoke his spell and the ox stood beside him, alive.

When the ox had been taken back to its stall
and all the blood washed from the floor, Khufu
ordered the keepers of the royal menagerie to
bring in a fierce lion. Muzzled and leashed, the
lion was dragged in by two keepers. Djedi
ordered them to release it and the keepers
scattered as the angry lion tensed to spring. Just
in time, Djedi murmured his spell and the lion
trotted to his heels and followed him around the
throne-room like a dog.

When the docile lion had been taken back to
the menagerie, Khufu beckoned to Djedi and
whispered to him, 'It is rumoured that you
know the number and plan of the secret
chambers of Thoth . . .'
'By your favour, Sovereign, my lord,' began
Djedi, 'I do not know myself but I do know how
to find out. In the temple at Heliopolis is hidden
a chest of flint and the plan of the secret
chambers of Thoth is hidden in it.'
'Bring me the chest,' commanded Khufu, 'and
you shall name your reward!'
'Sovereign, my lord,' answered Djedi, 'the man
is not yet born who will bring you the chest of
flint. The only person who can find it is the
oldest of the three children in the womb of
Reddedet.'
'Who is this Reddedet?' demanded Khufu.
'She is the wife of Rawosre, the priest of Ra,
Lord of Sakhbu,' replied Djedi. 'She will soon
bear three sons to Ra and they will all be kings of
Upper and Lower Egypt.'

When the king heard this he was sad and angry
and his courtiers trembled but Djedi said calmly,
'What is this mood, my Sovereign? First your
son will be king of Egypt and then his son and
then the eldest of the children of Reddedet.'

Khufu was still angry to think that his
descendants would not rule Egypt for ever but
he hid his feelings and ordered that Djedi should
live in the house of Prince Hardjedef and be
rewarded for his skill with ample rations.

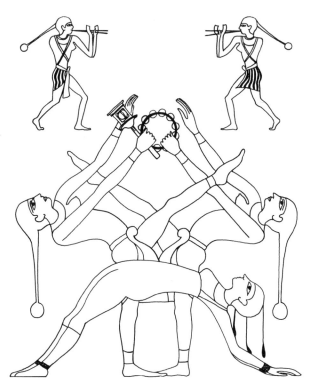

On the fifteenth day of the first month of
winter, Reddedet was gripped with the pain of
childbirth and lay on her bed for many hours,
suffering cruelly. Ra, Lord of Sakhbu heard her
cries and moans of agony and sent for Khnum
and Isis and Nephthys and for Heket and
Meskhenet the goddesses of birth.
'Go down to Egypt,' he said, 'and help Reddedet
in her difficult labour for her children will be
kings who will build you many temples and
make you offerings.' Then the goddesses
disguised themselves as a troop of musicians,
dressed in gaudy clothes and carrying flutes and
rattles and tambourines. Khnum turned himself
into their porter and took a birth-stool with him.
Then they walked by the house of the priest.

Rawosre stood in the doorway of his house,
unshaven and dishevelled. He was desperately
anxious about his wife Reddedet for the midwife
had not yet arrived from the nearest town. When
he saw the musicians and realized that their
porter was carrying a birth-stool, Rawosre
rushed towards them.
'Ladies, my wife is in childbirth and suffering
cruelly . . .'
'We know all about childbirth,' said the
goddesses promptly. 'We will help you.'

Rawosre quickly led them to Reddedet's room and was happy to leave them with her. Once the door was locked the deities helped Reddedet onto the birth-stool. Isis stood in front of her and Nephthys behind her while Heket hastened the birth. A golden child was born, already wearing a royal head-dress of lapis-lazuli. When the cord had been cut and the baby had been washed, Meskhenet held him in her arms and promised that he should be a king while Khnum breathed life into him. Two more sons, just like the first, were quickly born, named as kings and given life. Then the goddesses helped Reddedet back to her bed and placed the three children beside her. Reddedet's husband was waiting for them outside.

'May you be happy,' said Isis. 'Your wife has born three fine sons.'

Rawosre was overjoyed. 'Ladies, how can I thank you, what can I do for you? At least take this sack of barley as a small reward.'

Khnum slung the sack across his shoulders and they left the house but before they had gone far, Isis said, 'Should we really return to Ra without having done some marvel to report?'

So the goddesses made three precious royal crowns and hid them in the sack of barley. Then they summoned a heavy rainstorm as an excuse to return to Rawosre's house. Isis knocked on the door and asked one of the servants to store the sack for them or it would be soaked in the rain and the barley would swell and burst before they could get it home. The servant put the sack in a bin in the storeroom and Isis promised that they would call for it the next time they were passing. Then Khnum and the goddesses returned to Ra.

Reddedet kept to her room for two weeks and at the end of that time a feast was planned to celebrate the safe birth of her children. She asked her maidservant whether everything was prepared. The girl said that all the food and drink was ready except the beer, for the only barley in the storeroom was the sack belonging to the musicians.

'Use that to make beer,' ordered Reddedet, 'and Rawosre will give them another sack.'

The maidservant went down and unlocked the storeroom but as she opened the door she heard singing and shouting and cheering as if a king were passing. She fled back to her mistress and told her what had happened. Reddedet could not believe the girl and went down to the storeroom herself. Sure enough, the room was filled with music and voices acclaiming a king but there was nothing to be seen but jars of wine and lentils and oil and sacks of grain.

Reddedet crept round the room trying to discover where the noises were coming from. She soon realized that they were loudest when she knelt by the bin that held the musicians' barley. Reddedet untied the sack and found the three crowns hidden in the grain. For the first time she understood that her children would be kings. Reddedet put the crowns back into the barley and put the sack in a sealed chest. When Rawosre came home she told him what she knew. He was overjoyed at her news.

A few days later Reddedet quarrelled with her maidservant and gave the girl a slap. She was very angry and said to her fellow servants, 'Why should I stand for this? I've guessed her secret, I know that her children are born to be kings. I shall go and tell King Khufu and see what he will do about it!'

She set out for Memphis but on her way the maidservant passed the threshing floor where her half-brother was binding flax. She told him what she intended to do and he was furious at her disloyalty and gave her a beating with a hank of flax. The girl ran down to the river to bathe her wounds and a crocodile grabbed her and pulled her under.

Her brother returned to the house of Rawosre and found Reddedet sitting crying.

'My lady, why are you so upset?'

'Because the girl I brought up in this house has run away,' answered Reddedet, 'and she means to denounce me to Khufu and I am afraid for my children!'

Then the brother said, 'My lady, the girl came and told me her plan. I gave her a good thrashing and she ran down to the river where a crocodile killed her.'

Reddedet was sorry for the maidservant but her heart rejoiced to think that Ra was watching over his children. She knew then that the god would protect them from the anger of Khufu and that nothing could stop them becoming kings.

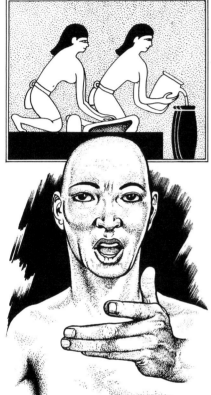

The eloquent peasant

Reddedet's children became the first three kings of the Fifth Dynasty (c2465–2323 BC) and the country prospered under their rule, but during the Sixth Dynasty (c2323–2150 BC) Egypt began to decline.

Many reasons have been suggested for the fall of the Old Kingdom. The climate seems to have continued to get drier and years of low Niles led to famines and weakened the people's faith in their kings. Unwisely, the Old Kingdom rulers gave away many of the royal lands to reward their officials and even allowed them to pass on their jobs to their sons. This made the civil service less efficient and more independent and was particularly dangerous in the case of the officials who governed the Nomes. These governors grew rich and powerful and began to rule their Nomes like petty kings. Wars broke out between them and for the century known as the First Intermediate Period (c2134–2020 BC) Egypt was divided and weak. The story of the eloquent peasant is set in this period when Egypt was full of corrupt officials but the old ideal of impartial justice was still remembered.

In the reign of King Nubkaure a peasant called Khunanup lived with his family by an oasis in the Western Desert. He worked hard all year round to gather foods to trade with in Egypt but he was still a poor man. One day Khunanup said to his wife, 'I'm going down to Egypt to barter for food for our children. Measure out what's left of our grain.'

When she brought the grain from their storeroom, Khunanup divided it into two uneven parts. 'Keep these twenty measures to feed you and the children while I'm away but take these six measures and make them into bread and beer for my journey.'

The peasant loaded his two donkeys with bundles of rushes, sacks of salt and natron, jackal hides and ostrich feathers. When the bread and beer were ready he said goodbye to his wife and children and led the donkeys south towards Heracleopolis.

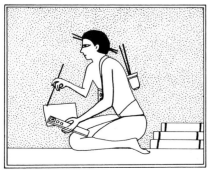

Some days later, as he was travelling through the district of Perfefi, Khunanup's donkeys were noticed by an official called Nemtynakht. This official was a greedy and ruthless man and when he saw the laden donkeys he decided to take them from the peasant. The house of Nemtynakht stood close to a narrow path which had a corn field on one side and the Nile on the other. The official sent one of his servants to fetch him a sheet and he spread it across the path with its fringe in the corn and its hem hanging over the river.

As Khunanup came along the path Nemtynakht called out, 'Be careful, peasant, don't let your filthy donkeys tread on the sheet I'm drying!'

'Whatever you say,' answered the peasant cheerfully, and he urged his donkeys up into the field to avoid the sheet.

'You wretched peasant!' shouted Nemtynakht. 'Now you're trampling my corn!'

'I can't help trampling the corn if your sheet is blocking the path,' said Khunanup reasonably but at that moment one of his donkeys seized and ate a wisp of corn.

'Thieving beast! I shall take this donkey,' announced the official, 'as payment for my stolen corn.'

'My donkey is worth far more than one wisp of corn!' protested Khunanup. 'I know that this estate belongs to the high steward Rensi. He is an enemy to every thief and he won't let me be robbed on his own land!'

Nemtynakht was furious with the peasant for arguing. 'It is me you have to deal with, not the high steward!'

He beat Khunanup with his staff and seized both the donkeys. The poor peasant sat down on the path and wept.

'Stop wailing,' snapped Nemtynakht, 'or I'll send you to the Lord of Silence!'

'First you rob me, then you beat me and now you forbid me to complain; but you can't stop me asking the gods for justice!'

For ten days Khunanup hung around the house of Nemtynakht, hoping to persuade him to give back the donkeys and their loads. When he saw that it was no use, the peasant walked to Heracleopolis to look for the high steward Rensi. He found Rensi standing on the river bank with a group of other judges, waiting for a barge to take them to the courthouse.

The high steward never refused a plea for justice and he ordered one of his scribes to stay behind and write down the details of the peasant's complaint. As they boarded the barge the other judges said to Rensi, 'Surely there is no need to punish an official for a few skins or a trifle of salt. The peasant probably belongs to him and has been caught trying to sell his master's goods.'

Rensi said nothing, but he was very angry with the judges because he knew that Nemtynakht was dishonest. It also saddened him to think how hard it was for a peasant to get a fair hearing.

The very next day the high steward read the details of Khunanup's case and summoned him before the court. Confident that Rensi was a just man, the peasant knelt down and began to speak: 'O high steward, greatest of the great, when you go down to the Sea of Justice, you shall have fair winds. No storm will strip away your sails and your mast will never snap. Truth will bring you safely to harbour for you are a father to the orphan, a husband to the widow, a brother to the helpless. You are free of greed, an enemy of lies and a friend of truth. You are a lord who hears the voice of the oppressed. Hear my plea, heal my grief, do me justice!'

Rensi, who was used to coaxing a few words out of silent or stammering peasants, was astonished to hear such an eloquent speech. He promised Khunanup that he would hear the case in full next day and hurried to the palace. Rensi bowed before King Nubkaure and said in great excitement, 'Sovereign, my lord, I have discovered a peasant who cannot read or write but who speaks with wonderful eloquence! He is a poor man and one of my officials has robbed him of his donkeys and trade goods so he has come to me asking for justice.'

The king was intrigued. 'As you value my happiness, Rensi, detain this peasant for a while. Be silent when he pleads and have someone write down everything he says. Make sure that he has enough to live on and that his wife and family are provided for. These peasants only come to Egypt to trade when their storerooms are nearly empty. Help them, but in secret!'

Everything was done as the king commanded. Rensi saw that the townspeople offered food to Khunanup and messages were sent to the oasis with orders that the peasant's wife and family were to be cared for. The next time Khunanup came into court, Rensi frowned and spoke coldly to him, but the peasant was not daunted. 'Great lord, justice is the rudder of heaven; you are the rudder of Egypt, the equal of Thoth who keeps the Balance and is the most impartial of judges. If you support the thief, who is there left to punish crime? The desperate can steal without reproach, but you are great and rich and powerful. Lord, be generous, be just!'

Rensi listened with secret pleasure to the peasant's speech and a scribe hidden behind a curtain wrote it all down. When it was over the high steward rose and left the court without a word and Khunanup went away dejected.

The next morning the peasant came back to the court and made a fierce speech attacking judges who were greedy or corrupt. Rensi said nothing but the courthouse guards gave Khunanup a thrashing for his insolence and Nemtynakht looked on and laughed.

For five more days the peasant came to court and pleaded his case but the high steward would not answer him. By the ninth day Khunanup was desperate. He knew that the rations he had left for his family would be used up by now and without him they might starve. The peasant went into the court knowing that if he could not get justice that day he would have to go home.

For the last time, Khunanup knelt before the high steward. 'Great one, do justice for the sake of the Lord of Justice and shun evil. When the just man dies his name is not forgotten on earth and his spirit is blessed in the Realm of the Dead; this is the law of the gods. Speak justice, do justice, for it is mighty and endures for ever!'

The peasant looked up at the high steward but Rensi was silent and gave him no sign.
'A man who once saw has now become blind,' said Khunanup sadly. 'A man who once heard has now become deaf. For nine days I have pleaded in vain, now I shall complain of you to the gods!'

He stood up and strode out of the court but Rensi ordered two guards to bring him back. Khunanup was sure that he was going to be punished for his bold words.
'When death comes,' he said steadily, 'it is like a cup of water to a thirsty man.'

For the first time the high steward smiled at him. 'Good peasant, do not be afraid. Stand there and listen to your pleas for justice.'

Khunanup was astounded when a scribe came forward and read out the nine speeches from a papyrus scroll.
'Come with me now to the palace,' said Rensi and the peasant soon found himself kissing the ground before the throne of King Nubkaure. The king read the speeches and was delighted that a peasant should speak so well and so bravely. He smiled on Khunanup and ordered the high steward to judge his case.

A terrified Nemtynakht was dragged into the throne room and beaten until he confessed his crimes. Then Rensi ordered that all the official's land and goods be given to Khunanup. So the eloquent peasant returned to his oasis a rich man and justice ruled in Egypt.

The shipwrecked sailor

During the turmoil that followed the decline of the Old Kingdom, a warlike dynasty from Thebes struggled to gain control of Upper Egypt. Montuhotpe, the greatest king of this dynasty, united the south and went on to reconquer the north. In about 2040 BC the Two Lands were joined again and the Middle Kingdom began. To renew the country's wealth, large expeditions were sent out by land and sea to mine for gold, turquoise and amethyst. A Middle Kingdom papyrus contains an exotic traveller's tale about one of these expeditions.

On a boat sailing downriver from Nubia to Egypt sat one of the king's most trusted officials, staring dejectedly into space. He was the leader of an expedition which, after a cluster of bad luck, was returning from the Nubian mines without its full quota of gold. He was just imagining what the king would say at the news of this failure when one of the other officials squatted down on the deck beside him.

'May your wishes be granted, commander. Just look at the crew hugging each other and thanking the gods for a safe journey home. At least we've crossed the Nubian border without losing a man. Listen to me! Wash, shave, put on your best clothes. When the king questions you, answer him calmly, without stammering. Then he'll know that you're not to blame. Speech can always save a man.'

The commander was in no mood to be comforted. 'It's no use my friend. Why waste water on a goose that's to be slaughtered in the morning?'

'Let me tell you about my first expedition,' said the kindly official. Settling himself down with his back resting against the commander's chair he related a strange story.

'My first voyage as a poor young sailor was across the Red Sea on a royal ship bound for the turquoise mines. We had a fine crew of one hundred and twenty men; the pick of Egypt. One day a sudden tempest lashed the sea and a giant wave shattered our mast. The crew did everything they could but within minutes the ship was sinking. Every man on board was drowned; except me. I was seized by a wave and thrown up on the shore of a strange island. 'I had just enough strength to crawl out of reach of the surf and into the shelter of a pile of driftwood. I lay there for three days and three long nights, exhausted and wretched, then hunger drove me inland. The centre of that island was like a garden. Birds sang in the branches of date palms and laden fig trees. Cucumbers grew in neat rows beside pools full of fish. Everything was carefully tended but there were no men to be seen.

My arms and my mouth were soon full of food and in my thankfulness I remembered the gods. With the copper knife from my belt I cut off a branch and fashioned a fire drill. When I'd got a fire alight I gathered up the remains of my meal to burn it as an offering to the gods. The moment the food was hissing in the flames I heard a thunderous noise.

'I thought at first that it was the roar of the sea but then the ground began to shake and the trees bowed and broke as if a storm wind was flattening them. When I found the courage to look up, it was not a storm I saw but a huge serpent. He was more than thirty cubits long and his golden scales were inlaid with lapis-lazuli. As he towered above me I fell on my belly and waited for death but the serpent hissed, "Who brought you here, little one? Tell me at once or I will turn you to ashes!"

'But I was too paralysed with fright to speak so the serpent picked me up in his jaws and carried me to his lair. He set me down unharmed and said again, "Who brought you here, little one?"

'I answered him without daring to look up:
"I was on a royal ship sailing with a picked crew to the land of the turquoise mines. A storm caught us and wrecked our ship. All my comrades were drowned and I am the only one left. It was the waves who brought me."

'Then the serpent bent over me and said in a gentler voice, "Don't be afraid little one, don't turn pale. You are safe with me. A god has chosen you to live and brought you to this enchanted island. It is full of good things and you shall spend four months here until a ship passes. You will know the crew of that ship and they will take you back to Egypt."

'A deep sigh rippled along the golden coils. "I understand how you have suffered, little one. Seventy-five serpents used to live on this beautiful island. They were my family, my sisters, my brothers, my children and, most beloved of all, the little daughter that the gods

sent to me in answer to my prayers. Then a star fell to earth and my whole family was destroyed in its flames. By chance I was not with them when it fell but when I found the charred heap of their bodies I wished that I had died too."

'I was no longer afraid of the serpent but I kissed the ground before him and said, "When I return to Egypt I will tell the king of your power and generosity. I shall send you scented oils and spices and incense. I shall tell everyone what you have done for me and sacrifice birds and oxen to you in my local temple. I will ask the king to send you a shipload of the finest goods in Egypt."

'The golden coils quivered again, but this time with laughter. "You are not wealthy, little one, and Egypt is not rich in oils or spices or incense, but I am the Lord of Punt, the Master of the Myrrh Groves and this island abounds in oils and spices. As for sending me gifts . . . once you have left this island you will never find it again."

'I was ashamed then of my foolishness but the serpent was kind to me and I lived for four contented months on his island. One day as I sat in the boughs of a tall tree I saw a ship on the horizon and as it sailed closer I recognized many of the crew. I scrambled down and ran to tell the serpent but he already knew my news and was drawing the ship towards the island by his magic. "Farewell little one," he said to me. "You will soon be on your way home to see your family again. Remember me kindly, that is all I ask."

'Then he gave me a cargo of myrrh and oil, spices and perfumes, elephant tusks, giraffe tails, hunting dogs, pet monkeys and all kinds of precious things. I kissed the ground before him and the serpent said, "Within two months you will be home with your family and you will prosper there for the rest of your life."

'Then I went down to the shore and hailed the ship. I embraced the crew and told them my news and we all praised the lord of the island. They helped me to load the precious cargo and we sailed straight back to Egypt, to the palace itself. I presented the myrrh and oil and all the other goods to the king and he was so pleased that he made me one of his officials and gave me land and servants. So, commander, do not despair, for we never know when bad luck will change and what the gods may bring us.'

The prince and the sphinx

The Middle Kingdom was brought to an end in the seventeenth century BC by the rise of foreign rulers in Lower Egypt. For a long time groups of people had been leaving Palestine and settling in the Delta and the biblical story of Joseph and his brothers should probably be set in this period. At first the settlement was peaceful and the foreigners brought with them new skills, such as bronze-making. They also introduced new types of sword and bow and the use of horses and chariots.

In later times the Egyptians called these foreigners the Hyksos and claimed that they had brutally invaded the Delta and oppressed the whole country. Certainly between 1640 and 1532 BC there were foreign kings ruling the north and exacting tribute from the south. The most powerful of these foreign kings were the 'Great Hyksos' who ruled the eastern Delta from the city of Avaris. The Hyksos adopted Egyptian ways and honoured Egyptian gods but before long a Theban family, the Seventeenth Dynasty (c1640–1550 BC) had begun to unite the south against them.

To begin with the Theban kingdom was small. To the south of them, Nubia had broken away from Egypt and had a prince of its own. To the north lay the realm of the Hyksos and the Thebans were forced to pay tribute to King Apophis at Avaris. The struggle against foreign domination lasted for three generations but slowly the Hyksos were pushed back. Avaris fell to the Thebans and the Hyksos king fled to Palestine. The Theban king Amonhotep I (1525–1504 BC) united Egypt again and pursued his enemy to inflict a final defeat, in

the process conquering most of the city states of Palestine. This was the beginning of Egypt's Near Eastern empire and the New Kingdom.

King Amonhotep was followed by his son-in-law, Thutmose I who completed the reconquest of Nubia and took Egyptian armies further north than they had ever been before. Under his grandson Thutmose III, Egypt won control of most of Syria and became the greatest power in the Near East. Thutmose III attributed his victories to Amon, the patron god of the Seventeenth and Eighteenth Dynasties. Amon began his divine career as the obscure 'Hidden God' of invisible forces, but when the Theban family who revered him became kings of all Egypt, Amon's name was linked with that of Ra and he was identified with the Creator, the King of the Gods. Amon-Ra, Mut his wife and Khons his son were worshipped at the vast temple of Karnak in eastern Thebes.

Thutmose III recorded his victories at Karnak and the temple walls are inscribed with lists of gold and silver, chariots, horses and slaves that he took from conquered cities and gave to the god. New Kingdom rulers were expected to be great warriors and Thutmose's son, Amonhotep II (c1427–1401 BC) was renowned for his strength and military skill. He was well over six feet tall, an enormous height for an ancient Egyptian and an inscription close to the great Sphinx at Giza records that Amonhotep excelled at rowing, archery and chariot racing.

The Great Sphinx of Giza is probably the most famous of all Egyptian statues. Carved four and a half thousand years ago from an outcrop of rock two hundred and forty feet long and sixty feet tall, it squats in the desert to the south of the Great Pyramids. The Sphinx has the body of a lion and the head of a king and the Egyptians came to worship it as a form of the Sun God called Harmarchis. The desert sands blow in great drifts around the Sphinx and the statue has often been almost covered by them. In 1818 European visitors to Giza cleared the sand away from the Sphinx and found a granite stela standing between its paws. The inscription on the stela tells of an encounter between the Sphinx and one of the sons of Amonhotep II.

King Amonhotep had many sons but handsome Prince Thutmose was the favourite of the people. Thutmose was stronger than all his brothers and a great sportsman. When the court was at Memphis, the prince liked to slip away from the splendours of the palace with one or two friends and drive his chariot into the lonely western desert. There he would amuse himself with lion hunting or chariot racing or with shooting arrows at a copper target.

One day Thutmose went hunting in the desert near Giza and drove past the Great Sphinx, but only its head was visible, all the rest was buried under drifts of sand. The noonday sun burned down on Thutmose and his companions and made them so hot and tired that they sought shelter in the shadow of the Sphinx. The chariot horses were soon tethered and Thutmose sat down on a patch of cool sand, leaned back on the stone cheek of the Sphinx, and fell asleep.

Immediately he was caught in a vivid dream. The prince found himself standing between giant stone paws and the voice of the Sphinx boomed out across the desert:
'Thutmose, my child, I am your father, I am the Sun God, I am Khepri and Atum and Ra, I am Harmarchis! Listen to me and I will give you my kingdom on earth. You shall stand at the head of the living and wear the White Crown and the Red Crown. You shall rule everything on which the eye of the sun shines. The tribute of all nations will be laid at your feet and you shall live long, because my heart has turned to you.
'All this will happen,' promised the Sphinx, 'if you will serve me. Behold, the sands of the desert are choking me and lie heavy on my limbs. Sweep them away before they overwhelm me and I will treat you as a son!'

When Thutmose woke he remembered his dream and hurried to Memphis to fetch offerings for Harmarchis. Within a few days, he had gathered an army of men to scoop sand into their baskets and carry it away. Gradually the outline of the lion body began to appear and the Sphinx was freed from the desert. Harmarchis kept his promises and Thutmose was soon chosen as Crown Prince. In due time he succeeded his father and throughout his reign Thutmose IV honoured Harmarchis and made offerings to the Great Sphinx.

The capture of Joppa

When King Thutmose III (c1479–1425 BC) came to the throne of Egypt in the fifteenth century BC, he spent season after season fighting in Syria and Palestine to extend the Egyptian Empire. The princes of cities conquered by Egypt were usually allowed to go on ruling as long as they bowed to Thutmose and paid him tribute. A story in a badly preserved manuscript tells how the Canaanite Prince of Joppa, the city we know today as Jaffa, rebelled against Egypt.

The beginning of the story is lost, but it is clear that news of the revolt had reached Thutmose and that he was anxious to crush it before other Palestinian cities were tempted to join in. The king could not leave Egypt straight away, so he sent an army marching north under one of his best generals, a man named Djhuty. To show that Djhuty was to be obeyed by the army as if he was the king himself, Thutmose gave the general his own gold and ebony mace.

Djhuty and his men sailed from the eastern Delta up the coast of Palestine until they reached Joppa. Then the army went ashore and quickly set up camp. Joppa was ringed by massive walls and the only gateway was flanked by towers manned by archers. Djhuty sent a herald to stand before the great gates and shout a challenge: 'Rebel of Joppa, surrender to the Son of Ra, the Golden Horus, the Strong Bull Arisen in Thebes, the Lord of the Two Lands, the King of Upper and Lower Egypt, Thutmose, may he be given life for ever! Surrender at once, or come out of the city and fight.'

The answer soon came back. The Prince of Joppa refused to surrender, but nor would he come out of the city and fight. He was too wise to risk bringing his men out into the open.

Djhuty had no choice but to order an attack on the city. With their shields held above their heads to protect them from the rain of arrows, the Egyptian troops advanced towards Joppa. They pushed tall ladders and wooden siege towers against the walls but the defenders clubbed the men who tried to clamber over the battlements and set the siege towers alight with fire arrows. After three hours of fierce fighting, Djhuty ordered his troops to retreat. Egyptian losses were heavy but the garrison of Joppa had hardly suffered at all.

That night he sat in his tent, wondering what to do next. There was little chance of storming the city and a siege might last for years.

Djhuty knew that he must try cunning.

Early next morning Djhuty sent his herald to the city gates with a letter for the Prince of Joppa. The soldiers on the walls let down a basket on the end of a rope and the letter was quickly drawn up and taken to the palace. The prince read the letter scornfully; it was only another demand for his surrender but then he noticed a message at the bottom scrawled in Djhuty's own writing. In it, the general admitted that he could not capture Joppa and because he was afraid of Thutmose's anger and greedy for bribes, he was prepared to come over to the prince's side. The message ended with an invitation to discuss terms.

A letter was quickly sent to Djhuty agreeing to a temporary truce and a meeting on the open ground between the city and the Egyptian camp. Just after noon the great gates opened to let out the chariots of the Prince of Joppa and twenty of his officers. Then the gates swung shut and were barred again on the inside.

Djhuty and twenty of his officers, all unarmed, met the Prince of Joppa and his men and invited them to sit down and discuss terms over a cup of wine.

Djhuty soon convinced the Prince of Joppa that he was sincere. 'My own wife and children are here in the camp,' began the general, 'but tonight I will send them into the city to stay in your palace as a pledge of my good faith. Tomorrow this army will be at your command, so let us drink to the freedom of Joppa!'

Everyone's cup was filled again and the warriors of Joppa and the Egyptian officers were soon drunk together. Only Djhuty drank less than he appeared to and was still sober. 'Send a messenger to Joppa to tell them the good news,' he suggested to the prince, 'but the rest of us have more to talk about and more wine to get through! Still, it's cruel to leave your horses standing there in this dust and heat. Let them be unyoked and taken into the camp.'

The Prince of Joppa gave the order himself and even agreed to go to Djhuty's tent for a private discussion of the general's reward. As they walked there the prince said, 'I hear that you carry with you the mace of King Thutmose himself. I should very much like to see it.'

Djhuty readily agreed and bowed the prince into his tent. Then he opened a sandalwood box and turned round with the mace in his hand. 'Here is the mace of King Thutmose, the young lion, Sekhmet's son. Rebel of Joppa, you shall feel the King's anger now!' Djhuty brought the mace crashing down on the prince's head, knocking him unconscious. The general quickly bound his prisoner with leather ropes weighted with copper and then sent a messenger to the Prince of Joppa's charioteer.
'My general has prepared gifts for the people of Joppa,' said the messenger, 'to show them that he is now their servant. Your prince orders you to escort the gift-bearers into the city and tell the Princess of Joppa to rejoice because the Egyptians have surrendered and send us tribute.'

The charioteer obeyed at once and drove the prince's golden chariot to the city gates with the gift-bearers marching behind him. Djhuty's gifts were packed in two hundred large baskets, each slung on a pole and carried by two men. The sentries listened to the charioteer's message. They could see that the gift-bearers were unarmed and that the prince's officers were still drinking with the Egyptians. Everything seemed in order, so they sent six men down to unbar the gates.

The gift-bearers marched in through the gateway and the prince's charioteer began to lead them towards the palace. Six men had started to push the gates shut again when the gift-bearers suddenly put down their baskets and tore them open. Egyptian soldiers sprang out, each armed with one sword for himself and two for his bearers. The sentries gave the alarm and fought fiercely but the gates were held open and Djhuty had already captured the prince's drunken officers and was marching his army to Joppa.

Within minutes the city was swarming with Egyptian troops and it was not long before the people of Joppa were forced to surrender or die. Captives were rounded up and the palace was stripped of its treasures. The next day a ship set sail for Egypt carrying rich spoils and the Prince of Joppa and his family as wretched prisoners. When King Thutmose saw them he praised the gods for the cunning of Djhuty and the capture of Joppa.

The doomed prince

There was once a king in Egypt who had no son. He visited all the temples in the land, making offerings to the gods, and begging them for an heir. At last the gods decreed that his wish should be granted. The king hurried back to his queen and nine months later a beautiful son was born to them.

That night as the child slept, rocked by nurses, fanned by pages, guarded by soldiers, the Seven Hathors came to foretell his fate. No-one saw them enter the palace, no-one heard their footsteps, but suddenly the seven goddesses encircled the child and gazed down at his sleeping face.

'He will die through a crocodile, a snake or a dog,' they said in grim chorus, and the Hathors disappeared as mysteriously as they had come.

The nurses fled to tell the king the terrible words of the seven goddesses and he was desolate. But the king was determined to save his son if he could, so he ordered a splendid palace to be built in the middle of the western desert. The baby prince was taken there with all his attendants. He was never allowed to go outside and he was seven years old before he even knew what an animal was.

One day, in his eighth year, the prince managed to find a way up onto the roof of the palace. From there he could look out across the red sands of the desert. The first thing he saw was a man walking along with a dog gambolling at his heels. The prince was fascinated and could not take his eyes off the dog. When one of his attendants scrambled up onto the roof after him, he asked at once, 'What is that following the man along the road?'

At first the man was reluctant to answer, but at last he said 'Highness, it is a greyhound.'

Then the boy said, 'Bring me one just like it,' and he set his heart on a dog; nothing else would please him.

His attendants did not know what to do and they went to tell the king. He was very alarmed but he could not bear his son to be unhappy so after a great deal of thought he said 'Bring the prince the very smallest puppy you can find, and that should keep him happy.'

The prince was enchanted with his puppy and played with it all day long. At first the attendants hovered over them, ready to snatch the puppy away if it tried to bite. But the puppy grew into a gentle and affectionate dog and everyone forgot the danger.

As the years passed, the prince grew more and more restless, and he began to see his palace as a prison. At last his attendants told him what the Seven Hathors had said on the night of his birth. They hoped that this would make him want to stay safely shut up in his desert palace. Instead the prince sent a message to his father saying, 'Why must I be kept here? If I am fated to die, nothing you can do will save me. So let me follow my heart, until the gods decide to take me.'

When the king heard his son's message he was very sad, but he knew that the prince was right. He sent his son a golden chariot, drawn by two white horses, a splendid sword, a bow and a quiver of arrows, and he told him that he could go where he liked. The prince crossed the Nile to the eastern desert, marvelling at all the new things he saw, but he did not notice a huge and ancient crocodile emerging from the river and lumbering after him. He drove his chariot on northwards, with his greyhound crouching at his heels. By day he hunted the desert animals, the ibex and the ostrich, the gazelle and the wild ass; at night he slept under the stars. Day and night the crocodile who was his fate, followed him.

After many weeks, when the prince's feet were sore, from standing up all day long driving his chariot, he reached the land of Naharin. Now the King of Naharin had only one child, a daughter. She had many suitors from the land of Khor and the king did not know how to choose between them. So he ordered a tower to be built, with a single window seventy cubits (about forty metres) above the ground. The king announced that he had shut his daughter up in the tower and that whoever could reach her window in a single leap should marry her. The princes of Khor gathered beneath the tower and day after day, week after week, they tried to leap to the window. None of them could jump so high, but they kept on trying for sometimes they would glimpse the princess standing at her window, and no-one who saw her could fail to love her.

One morning as the princes of Khor were exercising beneath the tower, the Prince of Egypt rode up and limped down from his chariot. The princes gave a kind welcome to the tired traveller. They bandaged his feet, rubbed scented oils into his wind-burned skin and ordered a meal to be served to him. When he had eaten and was resting in one of the tents that clustered around the tower, they asked him who he was.

The Prince of Egypt did not want anyone to know about the terrible fate hanging over him, so he answered 'I'm the son of an Egyptian officer. My mother died and my father married again. My step-mother hates me and I couldn't endure her cruelty any longer; so I've run away.'

Then the princes of Khor were very sorry for the young man, and urged him to stay with them. The Prince of Egypt gladly agreed and soon he was asking his new friends what they were doing gathered around the tower.
'For three months now,' answered one of the princes, 'we have been trying to leap up to the window of that tower, because whoever reaches the window will marry the King of Naharin's daughter.'
'If my feet weren't so sore,' murmured the Prince of Egypt, 'I would try the leap myself!'

The princes of Khor laughed. None of them thought that the young stranger was serious.

The next morning the princes of Khor tried again to reach the window. The Prince of Egypt stood at a distance watching them as each one ran forward, jumped—and flopped back onto the sand. Suddenly the Princess of Naharin appeared at her window. She could hardly stop herself laughing at the desperate efforts of the princes of Khor. Then she noticed a handsome young stranger standing among the tents. The princess longed for him to look up at her but he pretended not to see her.

For the next few days, the princess came to her window every morning. The princes of Khor were delighted; they did not realize that it was the stranger that drew her. At last, on the seventh morning, when the princess came to her window, the Prince of Egypt looked up and their eyes met. With a single leap he reached the sill. As he stepped through the window, the princess welcomed him with a kiss.

Her attendants rushed to tell the King of

Naharin that a man had reached his daughter's window. 'Which of the princes of Khor is it?' asked the king.

'It is not a prince at all,' said one of the attendants. 'Just the son of an Egyptian officer, who has run away from his stepmother!'

'What?' roared the king. 'Am I to give my only daughter to a fugitive, a nobody? Send him away at once!'

The attendants hurried to the tower and said to the Prince of Egypt, 'Go back where you came from!' They tried to push him out of the room, but the princess clung to him, shouting, 'I swear by Ra-Horakhty that if he is taken from me, I will neither eat nor drink until he is returned to me!' The attendants ran back to the king and told him what his daughter had said. 'Kill the stranger,' ordered the King of Naharin and soldiers broke into the tower, with their spears raised to stab the Prince of Egypt. Then the princess cried out, 'I swear by Ra that if you kill him, I too will be dead by sunset. I will not live an hour longer than he does!'

The soldiers did not dare to kill the prince and they went and told the king. He was very angry, and ordered that the princess and her suitor be brought before him. When the king saw the Prince of Egypt standing proudly before the throne, he was impressed by the young man's dignity and royal appearance. He sighed and gave the prince the kiss of peace.

'Well, if you are to be my son, tell me about yourself.' The prince repeated his story about the cruel stepmother and the marriage was celebrated that very day. The King of Naharin gave his daughter and her husband a splendid palace and they lived there very happily.

In the gardens of the palace was a lake and one night the crocodile who had followed the prince from Egypt slipped into its cool waters, intending to lie in wait for him there. Now a water demon lived in the lake and he did not want to share his home with the crocodile. Every day for three months the demon and the crocodile fought for possession of the lake and so for a time at least the prince was safe from one of his three fates.

It was not very long before the princess wheedled her husband into telling her the true story of his life. When she heard about the prophecy of the Seven Hathors the princess stared in horror at the greyhound sitting at her husband's feet and begged him to have the dog killed. The Prince of Egypt only laughed and said, 'What foolishness! I've raised him from a puppy, and I'm not going to kill him now.'

The princess said no more about it, but from that day she watched over her husband anxiously. One night, after a splendid feast, the Prince of Egypt fell asleep as soon as he lay down on the bed. His wife, however, stayed awake to watch over him. Suddenly a poisonous snake came out of a crack in the wall and glided towards the sleeping prince. His wife snatched up the flagon of wine that stood beside the bed, poured out a bowlful and set it down in the snake's path. The snake dipped its head into the bowl and drank up all the wine. The princess hurriedly poured out a bowl of beer. The snake swallowed that too and was then so drunk that it turned its back and could not move. The princess screamed for the guards and they rushed in and hacked the snake to pieces. The noise woke the prince and he sat up, demanding to know what had happened. His wife showed him the remains of the snake and said, 'Surely Ra will save you from your fates, he has already given one of them into your hands!'

Early one morning the prince got up before his wife and decided to go for a walk around his estates. His greyhound went with him, frisking at his heels. In a remote part of the palace gardens the prince paused to admire a lake fringed with palm-trees and stooped to pat his dog. Suddenly the animal snarled. Its eyes glittered as it began to speak, 'Prince, I am your fate!' It sprang at his throat and the prince fled.

The greyhound followed him, running as only a greyhound can. In desperation the prince waded into the lake and the greyhound, outwitted, paced angrily along the shore. Just as the prince thought he was safe the crocodile came up behind him and seized him in its terrible jaws. The prince almost fainted with horror as the monster dragged him to the bottom of the lake, but he found that could still breathe. The crocodile spoke: 'Prince,' it snarled, 'I am your fate! I followed you from Egypt to kill you, but

for three months now I have been fighting the demon of this lake. Help me to destroy the demon and I will spare your life.' Now when the demon returned . . .

Here, the only existing copy of the original story breaks off. We can never know for certain how the story ended when it was first written down over three thousand years ago, but it may have gone something like this . . .

Now when the demon returned, the waters of the lake seethed but a coldness crept over the Prince and he was unable to escape. Every night the demon left its lake to search for prey; early each morning it returned to the cool waters, for it could not endure the heat of the sun.

As usual when the demon appeared, the crocodile attacked its enemy. The demon gave a bubbling roar as the crocodile's teeth fastened on its leg. Its clawed hands raked the crocodile's back and the two enemies rolled in the slime on the bed of the lake. They fought fiercely but neither could really hurt the other, they were too evenly matched.

With the courage of desperation, the prince drew the bronze dagger that was his only weapon, swam towards the green back of the demon and stabbed at it with all his strength. However, the water slowed his thrust and the scales were too hard for bronze to pierce: the demon seemed to feel the stab no more than an insect bite. It turned its head and the wicked red eyes saw the prince. With the useless dagger still in his hand, the prince kicked out to propel himself upwards. His head broke through the surface of the lake but before he could strike out for the shore, the demon seized him.

All this time the greyhound had been running round the edge of the lake, barking and growling. The Princess of Naharin had missed her husband and she came out into the garden to look for him. When she heard the angry barking she knew that something was wrong. Calling a palace guard, she ran towards the noise.

The first thing they saw was the dog, baring its yellow teeth and growling furiously. At an order from the princess, the guard fitted an arrow to his bowstring and as the dog bounded, slavering, towards them, the guard shot it in the throat. It died instantly. The princess screamed as she saw her husband struggling with a monster in the middle of the lake. Hastily, the guard fitted another arrow but the prince and the demon were too close together to risk a shot.

One clawed hand tore at the prince's hair; the other gripped and pierced his shoulder. The prince stabbed at the scaly chest and pushed with all his strength, but the demon drew him into a fierce embrace. In a few moments he would be dragged down to his death. The prince looked up at the cloudy sky and prayed to Ra.

Suddenly the clouds parted and a brilliant shaft of sunlight struck the lake. Instantly the prince felt his enemy's grip weaken. The red eyes blinked against the dazzling light and the green scales seemed ready to melt in the heat of the sun. With a hiss of dismay, the demon released the prince, intent only on hiding again in the cool water at the bottom of the lake. As the green head sank, the prince raised his dagger and stabbed the demon through the eye. It gave one dying shriek and its flailing limbs knocked the prince backwards, thrusting him down to the bottom of the lake. The princess cried out in agony, certain that her husband was drowning and the guard waded into the turbulent waters to try to rescue him. To their surprise it was the crocodile that caught the prince on its broad back and carried him to the shore. The prince leaped to safety and into his wife's arms.

In spite of all that had happened the prince grieved for his dog and gave it a burial fit for a royal servant. He gave the lake to the crocodile and made sure that rich offerings were thrown into it every day. So the crocodile became fat and sluggish and never returned to Egypt. The princess and her husband invited the King of Naharin to a splendid feast and at last the prince related his true history. The king was delighted to learn that his daughter had married the only son of a ruler far more powerful than any of the princes of Khor.

Soon the prince and his wife travelled to Egypt to tell his father that he had escaped his three fates. The King of Egypt was overjoyed and vowed to build a temple to Ra. The prince and princess lived long and happily together and every day they praised the mercy of Ra, the only power greater than fate.

The two brothers

There were once two loving brothers named Anpu and Bata. Anpu was the elder and he was married and owned a farm. Bata came to live with Anpu and his wife and worked hard and cheerfully for them. He ploughed or reaped, milked the cows, gathered wood and completed a dozen other tasks each day. There was no-one to compare with him for strength and willingness and he was so wise in the ways of animals that he could understand their language. Every morning when he drove the cattle to pasture they would tell him where the lushest grass was to be found and he would take them there. So the cattle became fat and the whole farm prospered because of Bata.

One morning Anpu said to his brother, 'Yoke a team of oxen tomorrow and bring some sacks of seed to the field; it is time to begin ploughing.'

Bata did as Anpu ordered and the two brothers spent the next few days ploughing the fields and sowing barley and wheat. They were pleased with their work but when they came to the last field there was not enough seed left so Anpu sent his brother back to the house to fetch some more. Bata looked for his brother's wife, who was in charge of the storeroom, and found her sitting in the sun braiding her newly washed hair.

'Get up and fetch me some seed,' he said to her. 'Anpu is waiting and I must hurry back.'

Anpu's wife teased out a tangle with her deft fingers and answered without looking up, 'The storeroom's open. Fetch it yourself. Can't you see I'm busy with my hair?'

Bata went off to find a large container and then measured out enough seed to finish the sowing. He came out of the storeroom with a huge load slung across his shoulders, but his back was still straight and his walk sprightly.

Anpu's wife watched him through a curtain of hair and murmured, 'How much are you carrying there?'

'The weight of three sacks of wheat and two of barley,' answered Bata.

'How strong you are!' said Anpu's wife admiringly. 'Strong and handsome.' She got up and stroked the muscles of his arm. 'Come into the house with me, just for an hour. I promise I will be good to

you, and Anpu will never know about it.'

Bata dropped his load and backed away. 'What are you saying? Do you think that I would betray the brother who raised me? He's like a father to me and you should be like a mother. I won't tell anyone about you, but never say such things to me again!' He picked up his load and strode off to the fields.

Anpu's wife was furious with Bata for rejecting her but she was also frightened that he might after all tell someone what she had done. So she ripped her own clothes, worked grease into her skin to make it look as if she was covered with bruises and lay down on her bed to wait.

When the brothers had finished ploughing Bata went to drive the cattle home but Anpu walked straight back to the house. He soon realized that something was wrong. No fire had been lit, no food had been cooked and his wife did not hurry to greet him as she usually did. Instead Anpu found her lying on her bed, moaning and weeping. Her clothes were torn and she seemed to be badly bruised. Anpu knelt by the bed and demanded to know what had happened.

'When your brother came to fetch the seed, he saw me braiding my hair,' she sobbed. 'He tried to kiss me and make love to me but I pushed him away. I told him that you were like a father to him and that he should respect me as his mother. Then he was angry and beat me cruelly and said that he would hurt me even more if I dared to tell you what had happened. O husband, kill him for me,' begged Anpu's wife, 'or I shall never know a moment's peace!'

Anpu believed his wife's story and his anger was as fierce as a leopard's. He sharpened a spear and stood in the shadow behind the door to the cattle byre, waiting to kill his brother. Bata returned with the cattle at dusk and drove them towards the byre but the leading cow turned her head and lowed softly, 'Your brother hides with his spear behind the door. He means to kill you. Run while you can.'

Bata could not believe such a thing. He patted the cow on her rump and sent her into the byre, but when the next cow gave him the same warning he stooped down and saw his brother's feet behind the door. Then Bata was afraid and he began to run. Anpu pursued him, spear in hand, and anger gave him speed and strength. Swiftly as Bata ran, his brother began to gain on him. Dripping with sweat and gasping for breath, Bata prayed to Ra, 'O my good lord, who judges between the wicked and the innocent, save me now!'

Ra heard Bata's plea and caused a river to flow between the two brothers. The river was wide and deep and full of hungry crocodiles so Anpu dared not cross it. He was so furious that he struck his own hand for failing to kill his brother.

Bata paused on the far bank and shouted to Anpu, 'Brother, Ra delivers the wicked to the just, but we must be parted. Why have you tried to kill me without even giving me a chance to explain?'

'Do you deny that you tried to seduce my wife?'

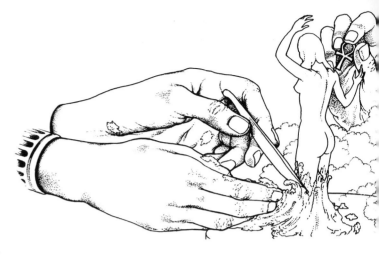

yelled Anpu, full of rage and pain.

'By Ra, it is a lie,' declared Bata. 'You have the story crooked. When I came back from the fields it was your wife who tried to seduce me and I who refused her. You almost murdered your brother for the sake of a worthless liar. By my own blood, I swear that this is the truth!'

In his distress, Bata took a reed knife and wounded himself. When he saw the blood gush out, Anpu believed his brother and was sick at heart. Bata sank to the ground, weak with loss of blood and Anpu longed to help him, but he could not cross the river.

'We must part,' repeated Bata in a feeble voice. 'I shall go to the Valley of the Cedar to find healing. Remember me kindly and listen now. I shall hide my heart in the cedar tree and if that tree is ever cut down I shall be in danger of death. If a jug of beer suddenly ferments in your hand, you will know that the worst has happened. Then you must come to the Valley of the Cedar and search for my heart, even if it takes you seven years. When you find it, place the heart in a bowl of cool water and, though I seem dead, I will revive.'

Anpu promised to obey his brother's words and went sadly home. He killed his wife with the spear he had sharpened for Bata and threw her body to the dogs.

Many days later Bata reached the Valley of the Cedar that lay in the desert hills close to the sea and rested there till his wound was healed. He lived by hunting the desert game and slowly built himself a fine house in the shadow of the great cedar tree that gave the valley its name. Among the branches of the tree he hid his heart.

He soon had everything he wanted; except a companion.

One day the Ennead were walking in the valley and came upon the house of Bata. The nine gods pitied his loneliness and Ra ordered Khnum to make a wife for Bata on his potter's wheel. When the gods had breathed life into her she was the most beautiful woman ever created, but even the Ennead could not give her a loving heart and when the Seven Hathors gathered to declare her fate they said with one voice: 'She will die by the knife!'

Nevertheless the Ennead were pleased with her beauty and they gave her to Bata. 'Your brother has killed his wicked wife,' said Ra, 'and you are avenged. Now, virtuous Bata, here is a wife for you, to be your companion in this lonely place.'

As soon as Bata saw her, he loved her and he knew that whoever met her would desire her. 'Stay in the house while I am out hunting,' he warned his wife, 'or the sea itself may try to carry you off and there would be little I could do to save you.'

Bata's wife nodded meekly but she soon grew bored with being shut up in the house and one day while Bata was hunting she went outside for a walk. As she stood beneath the cedar tree, the sea saw her and surged up the valley to embrace her. Bata's wife screamed and turned to run but the sea bellowed to the cedar tree, 'Catch her for me!' The cedar bowed down and its lowest branch caught in her hair. Bata's wife struggled free and fled into the house, leaving a single lock of her hair tangled in the branch.

The sea tore the lock from the cedar tree and carried it away to the very shores of Egypt, where the Nile seized it. Caressed by the river, the beautiful hair floated to the place where the royal washermen were laundering the clothes of Pharaoh. They dipped his fine linen tunics in the Nile, beat them on the rocks and spread them out to dry but the scent of the lock of hair had filled the river and it perfumed the clothes, too. When Pharaoh next put on a clean tunic he complained that it smelled of a woman's scent. The washermen protested that they had added no perfume but every day the clothes of Pharaoh came out of the river smelling sweetly.

One morning the overseer of the royal washermen paced the riverbank, making sure that everything was done as it should be. Suddenly his eye was caught by a shining lock of hair tangled in a clump of reeds. The overseer waded into the river to fetch it and as soon as he touched it he knew that he had found the source of the mysterious perfume. When the lock was dry it was taken to Pharaoh and he and all his court were sure that they had never seen hair of such a lustrous black, that felt so soft or smelled so sweetly.

'Surely such hair must belong to a daughter of Ra,' said the wise men of the court and Pharaoh longed to make such a woman his queen.

'Let envoys travel to every foreign land to search for her,' suggested the wise men, 'but we have heard that the most beautiful of all women lives in the Valley of the Cedar, so send twenty envoys there.'

Pharaoh was delighted with their advice and eagerly awaited the return of his messengers.

One by one the envoys came back from the foreign lands to say that their search had failed. Last of all a single wounded envoy returned from the Valley of the Cedar. Bata had killed all the rest when he had discovered their errand. The surviving messenger promised Pharaoh that Bata's wife was the woman he sought, so a great army was sent to fetch her. With the army travelled an old woman whom Pharaoh had chosen for her cunning tongue.

When they neared the Valley of the Cedar the old woman went ahead of the army and persuaded Bata's wife to let her into the house while he was away hunting. The old woman took out a casket of precious jewellery that Pharaoh had sent as a gift for Bata's wife. There were golden anklets, bracelets of lapis-lazuli, amulets of silver and turquoise; the old woman told Bata's wife that Pharaoh loved her and waited to make her Queen of all Egypt.

Greedy for the jewels and bored with her life in the lonely valley, Bata's wife agreed to go to Egypt but she was afraid of her husband's vengeance. Long before, Bata had told his beloved wife where his heart was hidden and now she used the secret to destroy him. The Egyptian soldiers were summoned and told to hack down the cedar tree. As it fell, Bata clutched his chest and died and his wife decked herself in Pharaoh's jewels and went with the soldiers. When Pharaoh saw her, his heart leaped with joy and he made her his chief queen.

At the very moment when Bata was killed, Anpu saw the beer in his jug bubble and froth and he knew that something terrible had happened. He put on his sandals, snatched up a staff and a spear and set out for the Valley of the Cedar. There he found his younger brother stretched out on the ground. Bata's limbs were stiff and cold and he no longer breathed. Anpu carried his brother into the house and wept over him, but he did not yet despair. Remembering Bata's words, he began to search for his brother's heart amongst the branches of the fallen cedar.

For three years he searched in vain. By the beginning of the fourth year he was longing to be back in Egypt and he said to himself, 'If I don't find the heart tomorrow, I shall go home.' He spent all the next day bent-backed amongst the fallen branches and, just as he was about to give up, his foot struck against something. Anpu thought at first that it was only a withered cone but when he took it into the house and lit a lamp he saw that he was holding his brother's heart.

Anpu put the heart in a bowl of cool water, placed the bowl beside his brother's body and settled down to wait. All through the night his heart swelled as it absorbed the water and when it reached its true size, Bata's body twitched and his eyes flew open. He stared up at his brother, still too weak to speak. Anpu held the bowl to Bata's lips and he drank the remaining water and

swallowed his heart. Then all his old strength returned to him and Bata leaped up and embraced his brother.

They spent the day talking over the past and planning revenge on Bata's cruel wife. 'Tomorrow, I shall transform myself into a fine bull of a size and colour that no-one has ever seen before,' said Bata. 'Then you must ride on my back to Egypt. When Pharaoh hears about us, he will want me for his own. Take the rewards he will offer you and go home. Then my revenge will begin.'

The next morning Bata changed himself into a huge golden bull with markings as blue as lapis and Anpu mounted on his back. As they travelled through Egypt people flocked to see the marvellous bull and when Pharaoh heard about it he gave thanks to the gods because he was sure that the bull must be their messenger. Anpu rode his brother to the gates of the palace and Pharaoh rewarded him with gold and silver, land and slaves.

Bata was garlanded with flowers and allowed to wander wherever he liked in the palace and its grounds. At first everyone was in awe of him but they soon learned to trust his gentleness. In all his wanderings Bata was only looking for one person and at last he found her.

One morning the queen herself was in the palace kitchens, overseeing the preparation of sweetmeats for Pharaoh. Bata came up behind her and touched the queen with the tip of his horns.
'Look at me; I am alive.'

The queen turned and stared at the bull in amazement. 'Who are you?' she whispered.
'I am Bata,' said the bull. 'I know that it was you who told Pharaoh's soldiers to chop down the cedar tree. You wanted me dead but I am alive.'

Then, as the queen stood trembling with horror, Bata paced slowly out of the kitchen.

In the cool of the evening, Pharaoh sat down to feast with his queen. She wore her filmiest dress and her finest jewels and as she poured out his wine, Pharaoh thought her more beautiful than ever.
'Sovereign, my lord,' murmured the queen, 'will you swear by the gods to grant whatever I desire? Do you love me enough for that?'

Pharaoh kissed her and promised that he would. The queen smiled. 'I desire to eat the liver of the great bull. He does nothing but wander about the palace all day, so why not slaughter him?'

Then Pharaoh was angry and upset at her request but he had given his word and the queen refused to change her mind. The very next morning Pharaoh proclaimed that the marvellous bull was to be sacrificed to the gods. The royal slaughterers seized Bata, roped his legs, threw him to the ground and cut his throat. As the bull died, his blood spattered the pillars on either side of the palace gate. The body was cut up and offered on the altars of the gods but the liver was cooked and given to the queen and she ate it with pleasure.

At dawn the next day the palace gatekeeper ran to Pharaoh's bedchamber and said, 'O, Sovereign, my Lord. A great marvel has happened! Two beautiful persea trees have sprung up in the night in front of the pillars before the great gate!'

Then Pharaoh rejoiced, sure that this was another sign of the favour of the gods; and no-one knew that the trees had sprung from Bata's blood.

A few days later Pharaoh and his queen rode in golden chariots to the palace gate and made offerings to the marvellous persea trees. Then thrones were brought and Pharaoh sat in the shade of one tree and his queen beneath the other while priestesses sang and danced in honour of the gods.

Pharaoh sat smiling but amongst the rustling of leaves his queen heard a voice: 'False one, you told Pharaoh's soldiers to cut down the cedar tree, you made Pharaoh slaughter the bull, but I am Bata, I am alive!'

Then the queen was very much afraid.

The next time she was alone with her husband the queen used all her womanly arts to please him and made him promise to grant any wish she named.

'Those two persea trees are useless standing at the gate,' she said. 'Have them chopped down and made into furniture for me.'

Pharaoh was uneasy at the thought of cutting down the mysterious trees but the queen sulked and wheedled until he agreed. The following morning she went with Pharaoh to watch the royal carpenters cut down the persea trees. At the first axe stroke, a splinter of wood flew up and entered the queen's lips and the moment she swallowed it she became pregnant.

After many months the queen gave birth to a handsome boy but she did not know that her son was Bata. Pharaoh loved the child and made him crown prince and as the years passed he grew up to be strong and handsome and wise. If the queen found that her son was cold towards her and noticed a growing resemblance to her murdered husband, she dared not speak.

In due time Pharaoh died and rejoined the gods and the crown prince succeeded him. No sooner was the coronation over than the new Pharaoh summoned the queen his mother. In front of the whole court Bata recounted the story of his strange life. He told of his flight from his brother's house, of the woman the gods had given him for a wife and how she had betrayed him.

'Surely such a woman is worthy of death,' said Bata and his courtiers agreed. The queen was led away, weeping, to die by the knife as the Seven Hathors had foreseen. Then Bata sent for his beloved brother and together they ruled Egypt for thirty years.

The blinding of Truth

There were once two brothers called Truth and Lies. Truth was noble and honest and his evil brother Lies hated him. One day Lies went to the Ennead and complained that Truth had stolen his dagger. When they asked him to describe this dagger Lies said glibly: 'All the copper in Mount Yal went into its blade and all the timber in Coptos into its haft. Its sheath is the length of a tomb shaft and the hides from all the cattle in Kal make up its belt. There never was such a splendid dagger before,' insisted Lies, 'and Truth has stolen it. If he refuses to give it back, let him be blinded and given to me as a doorkeeper.'

Truth was summoned before the Ennead and protested his innocence. He could not produce the dagger, since it had never existed, and Lies' accusations sounded so plausible that Truth was condemned. The Ennead ordered him to be blinded in both eyes and given to Lies to serve him as a doorkeeper.

Lies soon found that he could not bear the sight of Truth sitting patiently at his door. It reminded him every day of his own wickedness and his brother's innocence. So Lies said to two of Truth's old servants, 'Take your master out into the desert and leave him where a pride of lions is sure to find him. Don't come back until you're sure he's dead!'

The servants were too afraid of Lies to refuse. Sadly, each of them took Truth by the arm and they led him out towards the desert. When Truth felt the hot desert sand under his bare feet, he asked why they had brought him there. The servants wept as they told him about their orders.

'Don't leave me here for the lions,' begged Truth. 'Take me to some distant village and then stain my shirt with the blood of some animal and show it to Lies.'

The servants were glad to do as he suggested. They took Truth to a village half a day's journey away and then hurried back to tell Lies that his brother was dead.

Some days later a lady named Desire was walking in her garden when two of her maids ran up to her. 'Lady,' they panted, 'we have found a blind man lying in the reeds beside the lake. Come and see!'

'Bring him to me here,' said Desire.

The maids soon returned supporting Truth between them. He was exhausted and half-starved but Desire thought that he was the most handsome man she had ever seen. She welcomed him into her house and her bed and a son was born to them, but it was not long before Desire tired of her new lover. Then Truth was banished from the house.

The son of Desire and Truth was no ordinary child. He grew up tall and handsome as a god and by the time he was twelve he surpassed all his companions at school both in reading and writing and in the arts of war. The other boys became jealous, so they jeered at him, 'If you're so clever, tell us who your father is?'

The son of Desire did not know and he stood in miserable silence while the other boys mocked him until he could bear it no longer. Then he ran to his mother and said, 'Please tell me who my father is, so that I can tell the others.'
'Do you see the blind man sitting in the dust by the gate?' asked Desire. 'Well that is your father.'

The boy was shocked by his mother's callousness. 'And you leave him there? You deserve to be condemned to the crocodiles!'

He rushed into the courtyard and embraced his father. Then he brought Truth into the house and made him sit in the best chair. After he had set the choicest food before Truth and helped him to eat and drink, the boy said eagerly, 'Father, who dared to blind you? Tell me and I will avenge you.'
'It was my own brother,' Truth replied.

The boy quickly formed a plan and went to his mother's storeroom to fetch ten loaves, a skin of water, a sword, a staff and a pair of leather sandals. Then he took a handsome dappled ox from his mother's herd and drove it in front of him until he came to the place where Lies pastured his cattle. The boy approached the chief herdsman and said, 'I have to go on a journey. If you will look after my ox while I'm away, you can keep these provisions, this sword, this staff and these fine leather sandals.'

The herdsman readily agreed and the boy pretended to leave the district.

A few weeks later Lies came to inspect his herd. He immediately took a fancy to the handsome ox that belonged to the son of Truth. 'I'll drive that one home and slaughter it as a feast,' said Lies. 'It's easily the finest in the herd.'

The chief herdsman protested that the ox belonged to a boy who would come back soon to reclaim it. Lies shrugged. 'What does that matter? I'll take this ox now and you can give the boy the pick of the herd when he returns.'

So Lies took the ox away and had it slaughtered. The son of Truth soon heard what had happened and visited the herdsman.
'Any beast in the herd is yours,' said the chief herdsman. 'Pick whichever you like.'
'What good is that when none of them can compare with my ox?' asked the boy. 'My ox was so big that if it stood on the island of Amon its chin would be over the Nubian desert and its tail over the marshes of the Delta, with the tip of one horn resting on the Western Mountains and the other on the Eastern Mountains. If it lay down it would cover the Nile.'

The chief herdsman was astounded. 'Is there an ox as big as that?'

The son of Truth pretended to be very angry and he took the chief herdsman and Lies to court to be judged by the Ennead for the theft of his ox. In front of them all the boy described the ox again and Lies exclaimed, 'What nonsense, no-one has seen an ox as big as that!'
'No-one has ever seen a dagger the length of a tomb shaft,' said the son of Truth, 'with all the copper in Mount Yal in its blade, all the timber in Coptos in its haft and all the cattle hides in Kal in its belt.'

Lies turned pale as the boy cried to the Ennead, 'Judge Truth and Lies again. How could you condemn Truth on such a story? I am his son and I am here to avenge his innocence.'

Lies still protested that his original story was true: 'And if Truth is alive and can deny this, then I will confess guilt. Then you can blind me and make me his doorkeeper!'

Lies was confident that his brother was dead but the boy said triumphantly, 'You have judged yourself. Come with me now and I will show you all that Truth is still alive.'

He took the Ennead to his mother's house and showed them his father. When they had heard Truth's story they ordered Lies to be taken out and blinded in both eyes. After that Truth and his son lived happily together and Lies was their doorkeeper.

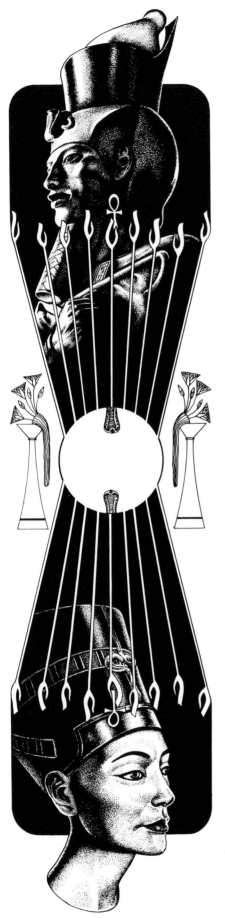

The Sun Pharaoh

In the early fourteenth century BC Egypt's empire seemed secure. Nubia was peaceful and the city states of Palestine and southern Syria had been subdued by five generations of warrior kings. However, when Amonhotep III, the son of Thutmose IV, came to the throne in about 1391 BC, he preferred the luxury of his court to the hardships of campaigning. He concentrated on building palaces and temples and made allies for Egypt by bribing foreign rulers with gold, or by marrying their daughters.

Amonhotep had a vast harem, but he seems to have been devoted to his chief wife, the forceful Queen Tiye. Although Tiye was not of royal blood, it was her son, another Amonhotep, who became Crown Prince. Amonhotep IV (c1353–1335 BC) proved to be the most extraordinary of all Egyptian rulers and he was the first to be called Pharaoh, a title that simply means 'The Palace'. More significantly he changed his name from Amonhotep (Amon is Gracious) to Akhenaten (Beneficial to the Aten).

The Aten was the disc of the sun and the young pharaoh believed that the sun god was the only deity who existed and that it was wrong to worship any other. Akhenaten built temples at Karnak in which the Aten was shown as a sun disc whose rays ended in hands holding out the sign of life to the pharaoh and to his lovely queen, Nefertiti.

Akhenaten soon abandoned Thebes and Memphis and withdrew, with his wife and daughters, to a new capital at el-Amarna called Akhet-Aten (Horizon of the Aten). Built on the edge of the desert, the city was filled with unique art and architecture. In an ordinary Egyptian temple offerings were made to a divine statue enclosed in a shrine inside a dark sanctuary, but in the temples of the Aten offerings were heaped onto altars built in courtyards open to the sun. The complex imagery of the old gods and goddesses was banished and statues and reliefs showed the Aten blessing the royal family. Portraits of Egyptian kings are usually highly stylized and full of remote grandeur but Akhenaten had himself shown as an ugly young man doing ordinary things like eating, drinking, playing with his little daughters and even kissing his wife. Shut up in his remote capital Akhenaten became more and more fanatical in his devotion to the Aten. He forbade the worship of other gods, closed down their temples, and sent gangs of men to hack out the names of deities such as Amon and the plural of the word god wherever they appeared in temple inscriptions. All mankind was to adore the Sole God and to honour Akhenaten as the living image of the Aten.

The events of Akhenaten's strange reign are surrounded in mystery, but it is clear that he made many enemies. The closure of the temples caused economic chaos and most people refused to abandon the old gods and goddesses. Akhenaten seems to have taken little interest in the running of Egypt and in the absence of a strong ruler law and order broke down. The empire was neglected, too, and many of the princes of Palestine and Syria seized the opportunity to free their cities from Egyptian oppression.

Akhenaten probably came to a violent end and his ideals did not survive him long. A ruler called Smenkhara had a brief reign after Akhenaten's death, but the identity and even the sex of this person is uncertain. Some historians think that Smenkhara was a younger brother of Akhenaten, but others believe that 'he' was none other than Queen Nefertiti. Akhenaten's chief wife played a very important part in everything he did and it is possible that he made her his co-ruler. She would not have been the first woman to rule Egypt; Hatsheput, the aunt of Thutmose III, had reigned as king for fifteen years only a few generations before.

Whoever Smenkhara was, he or she was soon succeeded by a new pharaoh, a boy of about nine years old called Tutankhaten. Though Akhenaten and Nefertiti had six daughters, they are never shown with a son. Tutankhaten may have been a much younger brother of Akhenaten or a son by a lesser wife. During most of the boy pharaoh's reign it was his Vizier Ay and the Commander of the Army, General Horemheb, who actually governed Egypt and who reversed all the changes made by Akhenaten. The young pharaoh altered his name from Tutankhaten (Living Image of the Aten) to Tutankhamon (Living Image of Amon). He returned to Thebes and the new capital, Akhet-Aten, was totally deserted, never to be inhabited again. The worship of the old gods and goddesses was restored and their temples were repaired and re-opened. The Amon form of Ra became once more the chief god and gradually Egypt began to return to normal.

Tutankhamon died suddenly at about the age of eighteen. Though he was married to one of Akhenaten's daughters, he had no children. The Vizier Ay took the throne and seems to have married Tutankhamon's widow, though he must have been old enough to be her grandfather. Ay gave his former master a hasty burial in the smallest tomb in the Valley of the Kings and reigned for four years (c1323–1319 BC). He was succeeded by General Horemheb who destroyed the temples that Akhenaten had built for the Aten at Karnak and completed the process of restoring law and order. Horemheb also died childless and left the throne to his elderly Vizier Ramesses, the founder of the Nineteenth Dynasty (c1307–1196 BC). Ramesses' vigorous son, Seti I, reconquered much of the empire and built splendid temples to the old gods.

The pharaohs of the Nineteenth Dynasty called Akhenaten the 'Great Criminal' and tried to destroy even the memory of his reign. The tomb of Akhenaten was desecrated and the names of the 'Great Criminal' and his successors, Smenkhara, Tutankhamon and Ay, were erased from the official list of Egyptian rulers. The treasure of Tutankhamon escaped the grave-robbers just because he was a forgotten pharaoh, buried in an insignificant tomb; and just because Akhet-Aten was abandoned to the desert, it is now the best preserved of all ancient Egyptian cities. When the court returned to Thebes under Tutankhamon, many things were left behind in the houses, palaces and temples of Akhet-Aten. Hundreds of clay tablets found in the remains of the Records Office proved to be copies of letters between the rulers of Egypt and foreign princes and the workshop of a sculptor contained his wonderful portraits of the royal family. Amongst them was a bust of Nefertiti which has made her famous as one of the most beautiful women of the ancient world.

The very people who tried to destroy the memory of the 'Great Criminal' have helped the names of Akhenaten and his family to live forever.

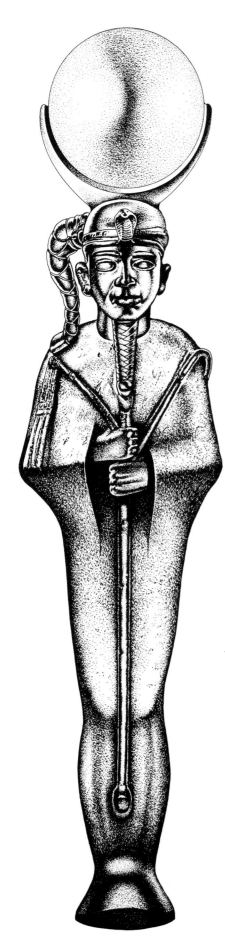

The Princess of Bakhtan

Seti I was followed by his famous son, the Pharaoh Ramesses II, who ruled Egypt for sixty-six years (c 1290–1224 BC). Like his father, Ramesses led his troops in person and he went into battle with his pet lion at his side. He fought hard to control Palestine and southern Syria but though his inscriptions boast of glorious victories, the truth is that the power of Egypt was kept in check by the rival empire of the Hittites. The homeland of the Hittites was the Anatolian plateau, now in Turkey, but during the late fourteenth and early thirteenth centuries BC they won themselves an empire in northern Syria. In the fifth year of his reign, Ramesses fought a great battle against the Hittites and their allies at Kadesh. Accounts of the battle insist that it was only the personal courage of pharaoh that saved the Egyptian forces when they came under surprise attack: 'My Majesty caused the forces of the Hittites to fall on their faces on top of each other, like crocodiles dropping into the river. I was after them like a griffin; I alone attacked all the foreign enemies, because my infantry and chariotry had deserted me. Not one of them looked back as he fled. As Ra loves me and as Atum favours me, everything my majesty says is the truth.'

Though Ramesses II may have fought like 'a raging lion in a valley of goats' both sides claimed Kadesh as a victory. Eventually Pharaoh was forced to make peace with the Hittites and Syria was divided between the two empires. The peace treaty, which still survives in two copies, seems to have been faithfully observed. Ramesses married a Hittite princess and devoted the rest of his long reign to gigantic building projects. He founded a new capital in the eastern Delta on the ancient site of the Hyksos city of Avaris and built many large temples, of which the Ramesseum at Thebes and the rock-cut temple of Abu Simbel are the best known. The quality of workmanship is often low, but in number and size his buildings surpassed those of any other pharaoh. He was worshipped as a god in his own lifetime and the Egyptians never forgot the splendours of Ramesses' rule. A thousand years after his death, a story set in his reign was written down in the temple of the god Khons at Thebes.

One summer Ramesses and his army drove their chariots through the land of Naharin, collecting tribute. The princes of the conquered lands hurried to bow before pharaoh and to bring him gifts of gold and silver, turquoise and lapis-lazuli. The Prince of Bakhtan longed to outdo the others and win the favour of Ramesses, so he offered the most precious thing in all Bakhtan, his oldest daughter. The princess was gracious, wise and lovely and the heart of Pharaoh was more pleased with her than with all the rest of the tribute. He gave the princess an Egyptian name, Neferure, and made her his chief wife. They returned to Egypt together and lived in great joy.

The following summer Ramesses was in Thebes, celebrating the festival of the great god Amon in the splendid temple he had built for him. As the final offerings were made, one of his courtiers whispered to Pharaoh that a messenger from the Prince of Bakhtan had arrived with gifts for Queen Neferure. As soon as he could, Ramesses sent for the messenger. When the gifts had been presented and admired the man kissed the ground before Pharaoh and said, 'Hail, sun who lights the conquered lands! O, Sovereign, my Lord, I have come to beg help for Bentresh, the sister of your Queen. She is ill and no-one in Bakhtan can cure her. Egypt is famous for her wise men's skill in healing. May your Majesty send us such a man to drive out the sickness that has seized our princess!'

Ramesses was eager to help. He consulted with his wisest priests and councillors and chose the royal scribe Djehutyemheb to return with the messenger to Bakhtan. It was a long and difficult journey but as soon as he arrived, Djehutyemheb was taken to the princess. Bentresh lay motionless on her bed. Her eyes were open but she did not seem to recognize her father when he stooped over her. As soon as the royal scribe touched the hand of the princess he sensed the presence of a fever demon of great power and malice. He tried to drive out the demon by chanting his most potent spells and covering her with amulets but with no success. 'Only a god would have the power to drive out such a demon,' said Djehutyemheb. 'Write to Pharaoh and beg him to send you a god from Egypt.'

The Prince of Bakhtan despatched a messenger that very day. After an exhausting journey the man arrived at Thebes during the festival of Amon. Pharaoh was shocked when he read the prince's letter. Such a request had never been made before, but because of his great love for Queen Neferure, Ramesses was anxious to grant it. He hurried to the temple of the great god Khons the Merciful and entering the dark sanctuary, he bowed before the divine image. 'My good lord,' began Pharaoh humbly, 'I have come to tell you about Bentresh, the sister of my queen. A fever demon has seized her and if it is not driven out soon, she will die. Of all your forms, Khons the Determiner is the most famous for healing the sick. Is it your will that an image of Khons the Determiner be sent to Bakhtan?'

The divine image nodded its golden head. Shivering with awe Ramesses asked, 'My good lord, will you strengthen Khons the Determiner with your power before I send him to Bakhtan to save the princess?'

The golden image nodded twice to show divine approval. Ramesses bowed his thanks and left the sanctuary.

Next morning Pharaoh sent four priests to carry the small gilded shrine that held the image of Khons the Determiner to the river bank. The image was wrapped with perfumed mummy bandages and hung with jewelled necklaces. Khon's single plait of hair was carved in lapis-lazuli and a silver crescent glittered on his dark brow. Ramesses gave the god a huge escort of priests, soldiers and servants, with boats for the journey down the Nile and chariots for the journey overland.

A year and five months passed before the stately procession of the god reached distant Bakhtan. At the news of their approach everyone rushed out of the palace to greet them. The Prince of Bakhtan fell on his belly before Khons, crying, 'Great god! Now you have come, be merciful to us as Pharaoh desired!'

Then the prince and his guard escorted the god to the place where Bentresh lay close to death. The priests set down the shrine of Khons the Determiner beside her bed and stepped back. The prince and his soldiers waited anxiously at one side of the room. The air became thick with magic and everyone sensed the unseen conflict as

Khons surrounded the princess with his protective power. With a violent convulsion, the fever demon suddenly left the body of Bentresh, hissing with rage and fear. The Prince of Bakhtan trembled when he saw the horrible shape of the fever demon hovering over his daughter, but Bentresh now lay in a peaceful sleep.

'Welcome in peace, great god,' declared the demon. 'Bakhtan is yours. Its people are your slaves and I am your slave too. Have mercy on me. I will leave this place for ever as soon as the prince makes offerings to me.'

The divine image nodded. The priests interpreted the wishes of the god and told the prince what he must do. Rich offerings were sent for and a banquet was spread for the god and the demon. The offerings were accepted and the fever demon left Bakhtan for ever. Then the prince woke his daughter and embraced her and the whole land rejoiced with them.

Bentresh and her father were so grateful to Khons and so impressed by the power of his image that they could not bear to let him be taken back to Egypt. The prince built a shrine for Khons the Determiner and kept him in Bakhtan for three years and nine months.

Then one night the prince dreamed that he saw the god emerge from his shrine in the shape of a golden falcon and fly towards Egypt. Dazzled by the glittering wings, the prince woke shaking with fear. He understood now how dangerous it was to cage a god and that Khons had chosen to return to Egypt.

The next morning the prince sent for the priests of Khons and said, 'Prepare to return to Egypt at once! Return to Thebes and I will send an army to protect you and chariots laden with gifts.'

Many months later the divine image arrived back safely in Thebes and the gifts of the Prince of Bakhtan were offered in the temple of Khons the Merciful. Khons the Determiner was returned to his sanctuary and Ramesses and his queen rejoiced to hear that Bentresh was healed.

The Book of Thoth

Ramesses II had over a hundred sons but his favourite was Prince Khaemwese, whom he made High Priest of Ptah at Memphis. Khaemwese was famous for his learning and for his interest in ancient times. A thousand years after his death the Egyptians were still telling stories which portrayed him as the wisest of magicians. One such story relates how Prince Setna Khaemwese discovered where the Book of Thoth was hidden. The Book of Thoth contained the most powerful of magic spells, and also the most dangerous, but that did not deter the royal magician.

One day, when the court was at Memphis, Setna went to his father and asked his permission to open one of the royal tombs in the City of the Dead. The whole court was shocked at such a request, but Setna explained that the famous Book of Thoth was hidden in the tomb of Prince Neferkaptah. Pharaoh tried hard to make his son give up such a rash idea, but when he saw that the prince was determined, he let him have his way. Ramesses knew that the dead could protect themselves and that Setna would have to learn to respect them.

The prince asked Anhurerau, the bravest of his younger brothers, to go with him and they took a gang of workmen into the City of the Dead. When they reached the ancient tomb of Neferkaptah, the workmen shovelled away the sand that had blown against its entrance. Gradually a wooden door was revealed. Setna broke the seals on the door and ordered the workmen to hack through the wood. Reluctantly, they obeyed. The rotten wood crumbled after a few blows and the tomb stood open. Setna and Anhurerau waited ten, tense minutes to let fresh air seep through the tomb, and then a torch was lit for them. None of the workmen would enter the black doorway, so the two brothers went in alone, Anhurerau holding up the torch and Setna a pace ahead of him.

They walked cautiously down a narrow passageway and through a shadowy hall carved with scenes of Prince Neferkaptah's funeral. Beyond, was a maze of small rooms and twisting passages. As they went deeper into the tomb, the heat and the stale air were suffocating. The light of Anhurerau's torch hardly seemed to penetrate the intense darkness and all around them there were rustlings and scratchings. 'It's only bats.' Setna had meant to reassure his brother, but his whisper echoed through the tomb and above them dozens of bats erupted into flight. As Anhurerau ducked, the whirr of their wings put out his torch and the darkness pounced. Setna froze. They would have to go back—if he could remember the way. It would be no use shouting for help; none of the workmen would enter the tomb. Suddenly Anhurerau gripped his brother's arm: 'Look!' Ahead of them was a faint glow. As the brothers moved towards it, the light grew brighter. Setna and Anhurerau crept round a corner in the passageway and found themselves staring into the burial chamber itself.

The room was crammed with rich furnishings; ebony thrones and vases of alabaster, stools draped with leopard skins and ivory caskets. On a golden couch lay the mummy of Neferkaptah, wrapped in scented linen, his face covered by a glittering mask. Beside the couch sat a beautiful woman, pale as a white lotus, with a little boy huddled at her feet. Light streamed from the scroll of papyrus that lay on a table in front of them, and Setna knew that he was looking at the Book of Thoth. Anhurerau stood trembling in the doorway, but Setna stepped boldly into the burial chamber and saluted the lady. The hand she raised to greet him was almost transparent, but her voice was low and sweet.

'Setna Khaemwese, why do you disturb the rest of the dead?'

'If you give me the Book of Thoth,' said Setna, trying not to sound as frightened as he felt, 'I will leave you in peace.'

The lovely ka shook her head. 'Setna, if you steal the Book of Thoth, it will bring you nothing but disaster. I see from your face that you do not believe me. I will tell you our story, and then you will understand the danger.

'My name is Ahwere. I was the only daughter of the King of Upper and Lower Egypt,' said the ka proudly. She looked down at the silent figure on the couch. 'I loved my brother Neferkaptah more than anything in the world and he loved me. I begged our father the king to let us marry and he agreed. A splendid feast was held to mark our marriage and we lived together very happily. It was not long before a son was born to us and we called him Mrib.' Ahwere reached down to touch the little boy who lay at her feet, and he

smiled up at her as if just waking from a dream. 'My husband was like you, Setna. He loved to wander in the City of the Dead to study the tombs or to visit temple libraries and try to read the ancient scrolls. He was a skilled magician, but he was always seeking more powerful spells. One day my husband attended a festival in the temple of Ptah. As he walked behind a procession, he read the spells written on the shrines of the gods. Suddenly Neferkaptah heard someone laughing at him. In the shadow of a column stood an old priest, amusement doubling the wrinkles on his face.

"Why are you laughing at me?" my husband demanded indignantly.

"I laugh at you reading such paltry spells," answered the priest, "when I could tell you where to find a magic book written by Thoth himself. There are two spells in it. If you read the first spell aloud, you will enchant the sky above and the sky below and the earth itself from the mountains to the seas. You will be able to understand every beast and bird and summon the fishes of the deep, just like a god. If you read the second spell, even if you are in the Land of the Dead, you will take your own form again and see the sun shine and the moon rise and the gods themselves."

'Then my husband flattered the priest. "Oh great one, may you live for ever! Name one wish that I can grant you, but tell me how to find the Book of Thoth." The old man's eyes glittered with greed.

"Give me a hundred silver pieces to pay for my funeral, and when the time comes, two priests to serve my ka." Neferkaptah sent for the silver and when the old priest had counted it he whispered to my husband, "The Book of Thoth is hidden in an iron box at the bottom of the river, near Coptos. Inside the iron box is a box of bronze and inside the box of bronze is a box of sycamore. Inside the sycamore box is a box of ebony and inside that, a box of ivory. In the ivory box is a box of silver and in the silver box, a box of gold and in that box, the Book of Thoth, and there are snakes and scorpions guarding all the boxes."

'Then Neferkaptah was dizzy with excitement. He rushed back to the palace to tell me

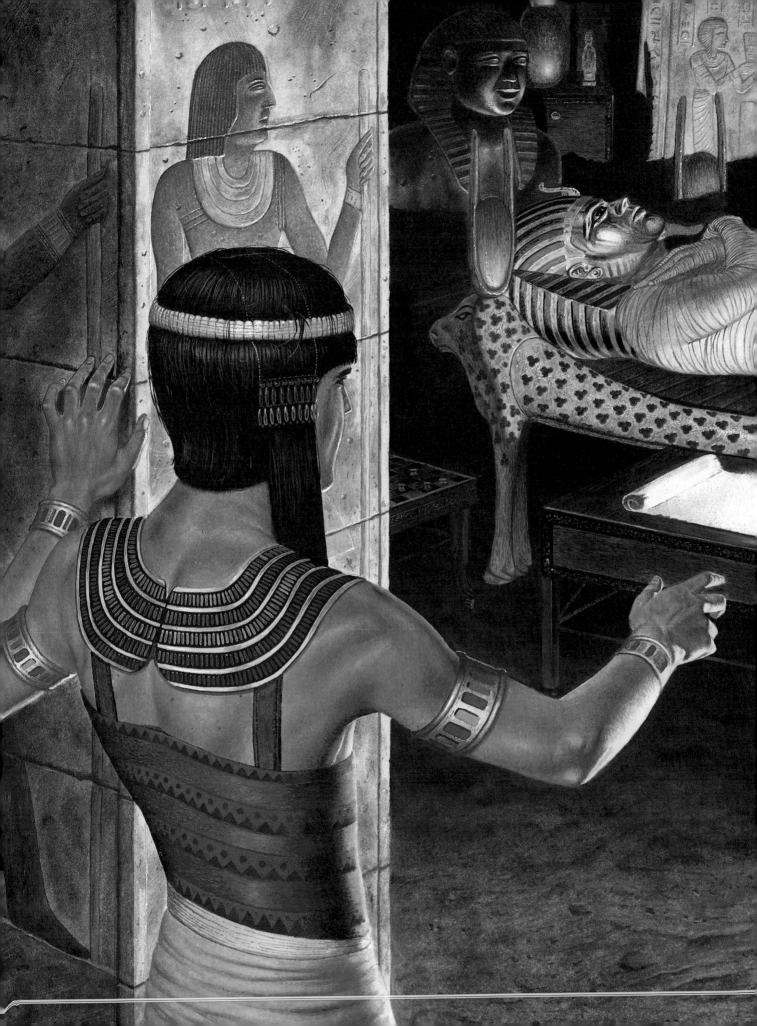

everything that had happened and said, "I will sail to Coptos at once and bring back the Book of Thoth!" Then I was afraid and I cursed that old priest. "May the gods smite him for telling you such a secret. I know that Coptos will bring us nothing but sorrow." I begged Neferkaptah not to sail south, but he could think of nothing but the Book of Thoth and he would not listen.'

Ahwere sighed. 'The king gave us a splendid ship. Neferkaptah sailed south and Mrib and I went with him. When we reached Coptos the priests of the temple of Isis and their wives hurried out to meet us and we spent four days feasting with them. On the fifth day my husband sent for pure wax and modelled a boat with all its crew. Then he crouched over it, muttering spells and breathed life into the crew. He launched the wax boat on the river and loaded the royal ship with sand. Then my husband went on board and I sat down on the river bank, determined not to move until he came back.

'Neferkaptah called out to the crew of the wax boat: "Row oarsmen, row to the place where the Book of Thoth is hidden!" The wax men took up their oars and they rowed for three days and three nights and the royal ship followed. On the fourth morning, the wax boat stopped and my husband knew that they must have reached the right place. He threw out the sand on either side of the ship so that the waters divided and there was a strip of dry land in the middle of the river. Neferkaptah went down between the banks of sand, reciting spells, for the iron box crawled with snakes and scorpions.

'The snakes hissed and the scorpions raised their deadly tails but my husband's spells were strong and the snakes froze as they tried to spit poison and the scorpions could not reach him with their stings. Yet around the iron box itself was coiled a serpent too vast for any spell to bind. My husband was not afraid; he stunned it with a blow from his bronze axe and chopped it in half. To his horror the two halves joined up again and within seconds the great serpent was coiling round him.

'Neferkaptah flinched from its poisonous breath. The coils tightened as the serpent tried to crush him, but he just had time to draw his dagger and hack through the glittering scales.

Again my husband cut the serpent in two, but as he staggered backwards the coils rejoined. Neferkaptah snatched up his axe and wearily attacked for the third time. He slashed through its coils and for a moment the serpent lay motionless. Then to my husband's despair the severed coils began to wriggle towards each other. With sudden inspiration, Neferkaptah picked up a handful of sand and threw it between the two halves. The snake struggled to join itself together again but now there was something between the halves the magic wouldn't work. With a frantic hissing the creature quivered and died.

'Neferkaptah kicked the body aside and wrenched open the iron box. Inside was a box of bronze, just as the old priest had said. Impatiently my husband tore open the boxes of bronze and sycamore, ebony, ivory and silver and came to a slender golden box. He lifted the lid and there lay a gleaming scroll—the Book of Thoth.'

Awhere paused. Her pale fingers touched the papyrus on the table in front of her but her eyes lingered on the mask that hid her husband's face. 'Neferkaptah unrolled the Book of Thoth and dared to read the first spell. He enchanted the sky above and the sky below and the whole earth from the mountains to the seas. He understood the speech of every living thing, even the fishes of the deep and the beasts of the desert hills. That was not enough for my husband and he read the second spell. By its terrible power he saw the Sun and the Moon and the stars in their true form and the glory of the gods themselves.

'Then Neferkaptah returned to his ship. He spoke a spell to the river and the waters flooded back over the scattered boxes, but the Book of Thoth was safe in my husband's hand. He ordered the crew of the wax boat to row back to Coptos and they rowed without pausing for three days and three nights.

'Now all this time I had been sitting on the river bank below the temple of Isis. I wouldn't eat or drink until I knew what had happened to my husband and by the seventh morning I looked fit for the embalmers. But at last the royal ship sailed into view and Neferkaptah sprang ashore. When we'd embraced each other, I asked to see the Book of Thoth and he put it in my hand. I read the first spell and the second and shared my husband's power. Then Neferkaptah sent for fresh papyrus and he copied down the words of the Book of Thoth. He soaked the new scroll in beer and then crumbled it into a bowl and dissolved it in water. He swallowed the water and with it drank the power of the two spells. We made thank offerings in the temple of Isis and sailed north again with Mrib our son.

'My husband was delighted with his success but the Wise One knew what Neferkaptah had done and he was very angry. Thoth hurried to Ra the King of the Gods and demanded justice: "Neferkaptah the son of King Mernebptah has discovered the hiding place of my magic book. He has killed the guardian and opened the seven boxes and read the forbidden spells! Such crimes cannot go unpunished." Then Ra gave judgement in favour of Thoth and decreed that we should never come safely home to Memphis. The three of us were sitting on deck beneath a gilded awning. We did not know that from that moment we were doomed.'

Ahwere's dark eyes filled with tears and Mrib covered his ears, as if he could not bear to listen to the next part of the story. 'Our little boy slipped away from the couch where I sat with Neferkaptah. As Mrib leaned over the ship's rail to gaze at the Nile, the curse of Ra struck him and he tumbled into the water. I screamed at the splash and all the sailors shouted. My husband ran out from under the awning and said the second spell of the Book of Thoth. Mrib rose up from the Nile, threw back his sodden hair and spoke. He told us of the anger of Thoth and that Ra had cursed us. No spell could save Mrib, he was already drowned. His lips closed and our son fell dead at my feet. We returned to Coptos and lived through seventy desolate days while Mrib's body was prepared by the embalmers and a princely tomb was made ready.

'After the burial we sailed north to tell our father the king the tragic news of Mrib's death. Neferkaptah watched over me anxiously but I paced the deck, grieving for my son. When we reached the place where Mrib had drowned, the curse of Ra struck me and I fell into the river. The waters closed over my head and I drowned

before my husband could reach me. Neferkaptah spoke the second spell and raised up my body. I told him of the anger of Thoth and the curse of Ra, but my ka had already passed into the West. My husband took me back to Coptos and I was buried in Mrib's tomb.

'Neferkaptah boarded the royal ship to sail back to Memphis, but he said to himself, "I cannot bear to stay in Coptos, close to the tomb of my wife and son but how can I go back to Memphis and tell the king 'I took your daughter and your only grandchild to Coptos but I cannot bring them back. I am alive, but they are dead'." My husband knew that he could not bear to live a day longer. He took a strip of linen and bound the Book of Thoth to his body. Then he leaped over the ship's rail and into the Nile. The sailors cried out in horror, but they could not even find my husband's body.

'When the ship reached Memphis, the sailors sent a messenger with the terrible news that both the king's children were dead. The court went into mourning and the king himself came down to the harbour with all the people of Memphis and the priests of Ptah. He saw Neferkaptah's body tangled in the rudders of the royal ship. The body was taken out of the water and all the people wept. The king said, "Let that accursed book be buried with my son." The body of Neferkaptah was taken to the embalmers and after seventy days it was laid to rest in this very tomb. Now I have told you how misery came to us because of the book you want me to give you. The Book of Thoth cost us our lives, it can never be yours.'

Setna was shaken by Ahwere's story but the light of the Book of Thoth dazzled him and he could not bear to give it up. 'Let me have the book,' he repeated, 'or I'll take it by force!' Then the mummy of Prince Neferkaptah slowly sat up and a voice came from behind the mask: 'Setna Khaemwese, if you will not listen to Ahwere's warning, are you a great enough magician to take the Book of Thoth from me? Or will you play four games of draughts? If you win, you shall have the Book of Thoth as your prize.'

At the chilling sound of Neferkaptah's voice, Anhurerau shrank back. What would happen if

Setna lost the games? He whispered to his brother to run but Setna stepped closer to the Book of Thoth. 'I am ready,' he said.

Close to the couch was a draughts board with squares of ebony and ivory, set with pieces of gold and silver. They began the first game, and the pieces moved without being touched. Setna was a skilful player but the dead prince was a better one. Neferkaptah won the first game and murmured a spell. Setna sank into the ground up to his ankles.

Anhurerau tried to pull his brother out, but he was stuck fast. There was nothing that Setna could do but play the second game; he lost that too. Neferkaptah murmured another spell and Setna sank into the ground up to his hips. Setna realized that he had staked his life against the Book of Thoth and the third game began.

There was silence in the burial chamber as the pieces moved across the squares. Setna played cunningly but the dead prince seemed to read his mind and slowly the game was lost. Neferkaptah spoke a third spell and Setna sank into the ground up to his chin. He could move nothing but his eyes and his lips. Setna whispered desperately to Anhurerau: 'Get out of the tomb! Run to Pharaoh and fetch my magic books and the Amulets of Ptah.'

As the fourth and final game began, Anhurerau fled back along the passage. As the light from the burial chamber faded, he felt his way along the walls, praying to Ptah that he would not get lost in the darkness. It seemed a horribly long time before he saw daylight again. Anhurerau burst out of the tomb, terrifying the nervous workmen, and ran to the place where Pharaoh was. When he had gasped out his story Ramesses said, 'Hurry my son, take Setna these books of magic and these amulets of power!' Anhurerau hurried back with magic scrolls under his arm, a torch in one hand and the Amulets of Ptah in the other.

In the burial chamber the silver pieces were already outnumbered by the gold; Setna was losing for the fourth time. It would be his last game; already he could imagine the earth closing over his lips, his nose, his eyes . . . Setna was not playing to win any more, only to delay the dreadful moment. Finally it came. Neferkaptah made the winning move and the words of the fourth spell came from the glittering mask. Setna was opening his mouth to beg for mercy when he heard the sound of running feet.

Anhurerau rushed into the burial chamber, knelt by his brother and placed the Amulets of Ptah on his head. Instantly the power of Ptah freed Setna from the dead prince's spell. He shot out of the ground, swayed for a moment and then grabbed the Book of Thoth. Setna and his brother fled from the burial chamber. There was no need for Anhurerau's torch, light walked in front of them, and darkness behind them. In the gloomy burial chamber Ahwere wept and Mrib clung to her.
'Hail King of Darkness,' she whispered.
'Farewell King of Light! The power that kept us together is gone, and I shall be banished to my lonely tomb.' But Neferkaptah had drunk the words of the Book of Thoth and he was far from helpless.
'Do not be unhappy,' he said. 'I will make Setna return the book himself, with a forked stick in his hand and a dish of incense on his head.'

When the two princes emerged from the tomb, they ordered the workmen to brick up the entrance and pile sand against it. Then Setna hurried before Pharaoh and told him everything that had happened. Ramesses looked grave. 'If you are wise my son, you will return the Book of Thoth at once or Neferkaptah will humiliate you and make you take it back, carrying the stick of a suppliant, with incense burning to protect you.' Setna was not listening; he could not wait to unroll the gleaming papyrus.

For several days he studied the scroll, learning to read the ancient script. One morning Setna paced the courtyard of the temple of Ptah, pondering the words of the first spell. Suddenly he saw a woman walking towards the inner temple with a great crowd of maids and pages. From her dainty sandalled feet to her shining braids of blue-black hair, she was the loveliest creature that Setna had ever seen. For a moment their eyes met and he hardly knew where he was. Then the woman hid her face behind an ostrich-feather fan and walked on.

Setna called to one of his slaves, 'Did you see that woman? Find out who she is!' He waited impatiently in the shadow of the temple gateway until the boy returned.
'My Lord, her maids tell me that she is the Lady Tabube, the daughter of the Prophet of Bastet of Ankhtawy, and she has come here to pray to Ptah.'
'Go back and speak to one of her maids, saying that Setna Khaemwese sends you. Ask her to tell her mistress that she shall have ten gold pieces, or a law case settled in her favour, if she will come and spend some time with me.'

The slave was very surprised at his master's words but he hastened to obey. Tabube was in the next courtyard making offerings of wine and flowers before the statue of Ptah. The slave edged up to one of her maids and whispered his master's offer. The maid was most indignant at such an insult to her mistress and railed at the poor slave. Tabube soon asked what the matter was and, with great embarrassment, the boy repeated the message. Tabube did not seem angry.

'Tell Setna Khaemwese,' she said, 'that I am a priestess and a lady of rank. If he wants to meet me, he must visit my house in Bubastis and I will entertain him there.' The boy hurried back to tell his master and Setna was delighted. He forgot all about his wife and family, he even forgot about the Book of Thoth. He could think of nothing but Tabube and the very next day he sailed north to Bubastis.

He soon found the house of the Prophet of Bastet of Ankhtawy and was asked to wait in the walled garden. Setna walked through a grove of fig trees and sat in a vine arbour, thinking about Tabube. Suddenly, he looked up and she was there. Tabube wore a clinging dress of transparent linen. Her eyelids were green with malachite, her lashes dark with kohl and her hair scented by lotus flowers.

She beckoned to Setna and took him inside the house to an upper chamber. The floor was of polished lapis and the walls were inlaid with turquoise. Ebony couches were draped with soft linen and a table was spread with dishes of pomegranates and vessels of wine. The air was thick with incense. Tabube drew Setna down beside her. She offered him fruit but he was too excited to eat. Tabube poured out the strong red wine and they drank together.

Setna longed to kiss her, but Tabube said, 'I am a priestess, a lady of rank. You ought to marry me and draw up a proper contract.' Setna was too infatuated to think twice about it. 'Send for a scribe,' he said. Almost at once a scribe appeared with a contract drawn up which made over all of Setna's wealth to his new wife. He signed it quickly and as soon as the scribe was gone, Setna tried to kiss Tabube again; but she drew back.

'That contract won't be valid unless your children agree to give up their rights. They are downstairs now, have them sent up so that they can sign our marriage contract.' Setna was too intoxicated by the strong wine and Tabube's beauty to think this odd. His little daughters were brought up and meekly signed the contract

that robbed them of their inheritance. When they had gone, Setna drank another goblet of wine and put his arms around Tabube's waist. She slipped out of his embrace and a tear shone on her rouged cheek.

'If you really love me,' she said, 'you will have your children killed. I am sure they will contest our marriage and make us unhappy.'

When Setna looked into Tabube's eyes, he could deny her nothing. He gave an order for his daughters to be killed and their bodies were thrown from the window into a courtyard. Setna could hear dogs and cats tearing at their bodies as he sat drinking with the beautiful Tabube. Then she put her white arms around his neck and leaned forward to kiss him. Suddenly Tabube's lips opened in a scream and Setna found himself crouching in the middle of a public road, embracing the dust. Tabube and her house had vanished. His head cleared and Setna realized the terrible thing that he had done. He moaned and grovelled in the dust. Passing travellers stared at him, wondering if he was drunk or mad.

Poor Setna did not notice the approach of four Nubians carrying an ebony chair. In the chair sat a man, dressed in splendid robes and wearing royal jewels. He seemed amused by Setna's plight.

'What is Prince Setna Khaemwese doing here in such a state?'

101

'Neferkaptah has done this to me,' said Setna bitterly. 'he has had his revenge and my children, my lovely daughters . . .'

The royal stranger smiled. 'Go back to Memphis. You will find your daughters safe and sound at Pharaoh's court.'

Setna could hardly believe his ears. Had it all been an illusion? The royal stranger nodded to one of his slaves, who tossed Setna a cloak to cover his filthy clothes. 'Go back to Memphis. Your children are safe,' he repeated. There was something familiar about the stranger's voice but before Setna could thank him, the chair and the Nubians and the stranger himself had vanished.

Setna rushed back to Memphis and his wife and daughters were surprised to be hugged so ardently and asked a dozen times if they were safe and well. That same day, Setna had an uncomfortable audience with Pharaoh. When he had related the whole story, Ramesses said, 'Setna, I tried to warn you but you would not listen. Now will you take back the Book of Thoth before anything worse happens?'

Later that day, workmen reopened the tomb of Neferkaptah. A shamefaced Setna walked through the doorway with a dish of incense balanced on his head, a forked stick in one hand and the Book of Thoth in the other. As he entered the burial chamber, Ahwere whispered, 'Ah Setna, you would never have escaped with your life without the blessing of Ptah!' But her husband laughed. 'So, my prophecy has come true.'

Setna bowed humbly to the dead prince and replaced the Book of Thoth. It lit the tomb like the rising sun.

'Is there anything else I must do?' asked Setna warily. Neferkaptah looked at the pale figures of his wife and son.

'By the strength of my magic,' he said, 'I keep the kas of my family close to me, but the task wearies me. Bring me their bodies from Coptos; then we shall be truly united.'

Setna left the tomb and told Pharaoh about the dead prince's request. Ramesses ordered a ship to be fitted out for the journey south. When Setna reached Coptos he was greeted by the priests of the temple of Isis and he offered oxen, geese and wine to the goddess and to Horus her son. Next day he went with the High Priest of Isis to the City of the Dead to search for the tomb of Mrib and Ahwere. He spent three days wandering among the tombs, turning over the ancient stones and reading the inscriptions, but none of them belonged to the family of Neferkaptah.

From distant Memphis the dead prince watched the search and when he saw that Setna could not find the tomb he turned himself into a very ancient priest and hobbled across the hillside. Setna greeted him courteously. 'You seem the most ancient man I've met in Coptos. Can you remember anything about the resting place of the Princess Ahwere and her son?'

The old man pretended to think for a while and then said, 'The grandfather of the grandfather of my father once said that the grandfather of his father had told him that the tomb of Ahwere lay there, under the southern corner of the house of the High Priest.'

Setna looked doubtful. 'How do I know that you're telling the truth? Perhaps you have a grudge against the High Priest and would like to see his house pulled down?'
'Keep me a prisoner while you pull the house down,' answered the old man with a toothless grin. 'And if you don't find the tomb, put me to death.'

Then Setna ordered his men to tear down the High Priest's house and under the southern corner they found an ancient tomb. At the bottom of a deep shaft were the coffins of Ahwere and Mrib. Setna had them reverently carried on board his ship. He ordered his men to start rebuilding the High Priest's house but when he went to reward the old man, he found the guards in confusion; their prisoner had vanished. Setna understood then who the old man must have been.

Setna sailed north and when they reached Memphis Pharaoh and all his court came to the harbour to honour the royal dead. The coffins of Ahwere and Mrib were carried into the burial chamber of Neferkaptah and the family were reunited. Setna himself saw the entrance bricked up. The tomb of the dead prince was never entered again and no-one else has read the Book of Thoth.

The young magician

Prince Setna Khaemwese and his wife Mehusekhe had two pretty daughters, but they longed for a son. Year after year they heaped the altars of the gods with rich offerings, but their prayers were never answered. Now at many Egyptian temples it was the custom for sick people and barren women to sleep in the sacred precincts. Every night they would lie down hoping that the deity would appear to them in a dream and tell them how they could be cured. In desperation, Setna decided to take his wife to spend the night in the temple of Osiris.

They arrived at dusk to find that the building meant to house the sick was already crowded and that many people were unrolling their bedding in the temple courtyard. Because of her high rank a room was found for Setna's wife, but it was no more than a narrow cubicle with thin walls. The Prince kissed Mehusekhe goodbye and left. She lay down on the strange bed and closed her eyes. The groans of the sick and the tearful prayers of barren women came from every side. Mehusekhe was sure that she would never be able to sleep in such a place, but she murmured a prayer to Isis and Osiris and after three tense hours she finally slept.

Just before dawn, Mehusekhe woke up, knowing that a god had spoken to her in her sleep. She could not remember what form the god had taken but she was sure that a mysterious voice had whispered, 'Wife of Setna, tomorrow you must go to the place where your husband bathes. The pool is overhung by a melon vine. Break off a branch with its fruit. Cut it up; grind it small; mix it with water and drink it down. Then embrace your husband and you will conceive a son.'

Mehusekhe made a thank offering, left the temple and hurried to find the pool and the melon vine. She did everything that the god had commanded and it was not long before she knew that she was pregnant. When she told Setna he was overjoyed and anxious all at once. He hung a powerful amulet around her neck and recited spells over her to keep her and her unborn child safe. One night a god came to Setna in his dreams and said, 'Setna Khaemwese, your wife is carrying a son. When the boy is born you must call him Sa-Osiris and he will do many wonders in Egypt.'

Setna woke from his dream even happier than before and impatient for the months of waiting to be over.

When her time came, Mehusekhe gave birth to a fine boy and Setna named him Sa-Osiris. It soon became clear that this was no ordinary child. When he was a year old, strangers always took him for a boy of two and when he was two everyone thought he was three. Setna watched over his son with pride and loved him dearly and Sa-Osiris was sent to school at an age when other children could hardly talk. He learned to read and write so quickly that within a few months he knew more than the elderly scribe who was his teacher.

Next, the boy was taken to the temple of Ptah, where his father was high priest, and placed in the care of the wise men in the House of Life. It was there that priests studied astronomy and mathematics, medicine and magic and made copies of the sacred books. Sa-Osiris was the most brilliant pupil that they had ever had. He learned the proper ritual for every god in every temple on every day of the year; he learned to name the stars and how to calculate which were lucky and which were unlucky days; he learned spells for driving out all kinds of sickness and for protecting the living and the dead. By the time he was seven he knew each book in the temple library by heart. Everyone who met him was amazed at the boy's cleverness and Setna looked forward to the day when he would present his marvellous son at court.

Late one afternoon Sa-Osiris and his father were together in their house in Memphis, dressing for a banquet. Setna was startled by a sudden wailing and, looking down from his window, he saw the funeral procession of a rich man. A gilded coffin on a sledge was dragged by a pair of oxen and surrounded by weeping women. With their bare feet, unbraided hair and torn clothes, the women were a picture of misery and they had been paid to beat their breasts and wail as loudly as if Osiris himself had just died again. Behind them walked lines of servants carrying ebony chairs, ivory caskets crammed with jewels, ostrich feather fans, chests of fine linen and many other precious things to be buried with the rich man in his splendid tomb.

Following after was another funeral. Wrapped in a mat, a poor man who had died homeless and friendless was being dragged to his shallow grave in the desert sand. He had no mourners to weep for him and not even a pot or a string of beads to be buried with him.
'By Ptah!' exclaimed Setna, 'how much happier the rich man is, even in death, than that poor wretch.'

Sa-Osiris came to the window to stand beside his father and said quietly, 'Do you think so? I only wish that you may share the fate of that poor man.'

Setna was surprised and hurt. 'How can you say such a thing?'
'If you like, father, I will show you what has happened to the rich man whom the mourners wail for and to the poor man who has no mourners. Come with me.'

With a secretive smile, Sa-Osiris gripped Setna's hand and led him out into the street. They took a ferry across the Nile and entered the City of the Dead on the edge of the western desert. As they stood amongst the ancient tombs, Sa-Osiris uttered a spell of grim power to break down the barriers between the realms of the living and the dead. Setna suddenly felt as if the weight of his body had dropped away and

that he could fly. At a dizzying speed the young magician swept his father past the gates of the Underworld. Setna glimpsed the shadowy forms of demons with long knives in their hands but Sa-Osiris knew the proper spells to appease the Guardians of the Gateways. They plunged deeper into the Underworld and when their pace slowed, Setna found himself looking down on a group of men who were squatting on the floor of a gloomy hall trying to plait straw into ropes. Their fingers were raw and their task could never be finished, for a donkey stood at each man's shoulder, eating the straw rope.

There were other men in the hall with jutting bones and faces gaunt with hunger. They were scrabbling to reach the loaves of bread and jugs of water that hung above their heads. Whenever it looked as if they would succeed, demons dug pits at their feet. The wretched men slipped down before they could grasp the food and water and they wept and cursed in their torment and hunger.

The next hall was full of souls pleading for mercy and the pivot of the great door was fixed in the eye of a man who continually wailed and prayed. Setna shuddered as the door swung open and the man screamed in agony, but Sa-Osiris swept them on into another hall. There the

demons of the Underworld were listing the sins of the newly dead in front of the Forty-Two Judges. In the last hall, Setna was dazzled by the mysterious form of the King of the Dead.

Shrouded in white linen, green-skinned Osiris sat beneath a golden canopy holding the crook and the flail, the symbols of kingship. Brave Isis and gentle Nephthys stood behind him and in front of him were jackal-headed Anubis, the guardian of the dead and ibis-headed Thoth, the scribe of the gods. The huge hall was filled with the spirits of the blessed dead and at its centre stood the scales that weighed the hearts of the dead against the feather of Truth. In the shadows squatted a monstrous shape, part lion, part crocodile, part hippopotamus; the shape of the Devourer who gave wicked souls a second death.

Sa-Osiris whispered to his awe-struck father, 'Do you see that blessed spirit who is clothed in golden raiments, who wears the feathers of Truth in his hair and who stands close to the throne of Osiris? That spirit is the poor man, whom you saw carried to a beggar's grave with no-one to mourn for him. His spirit entered the Underworld and was brought to the Place of Judgement. He faced the Forty-Two Judges and his heart was weighed against Truth. His good deeds were found to outweigh his bad deeds in the life that Thoth had allotted to him. Osiris himself ordered that the poor man should be given all the goods buried with the rich man and a place among the blessed spirits.'

Setna gazed in wonder at the shining spirit who only a few hours before had been a beggar on the streets of Memphis. Before he could form his next question, Sa-Osiris began to answer it. 'As for the rich man whose fine funeral you saw . . . in spite of his many chances to be generous to the poor and merciful to the weak, his bad deeds were far greater than his good deeds. Osiris condemned him to imprisonment in the Underworld. He is the wretched soul you saw with the pivot of a door fixed in his eye. By Osiris, the Lord of the Dead, when I said that I wanted you to share the poor man's fate, I knew what would happen to the two souls.'

Then Setna understood that he had misjudged his son and he humbly asked him to explain the other marvels which they had seen.

'The men you saw plaiting ropes that they could never complete and the men striving for food that they could never reach are wicked souls, condemned to torment. Dearest father, take the lesson to heart. If you are kind and gentle on earth, the King of the Dead will be kind and gentle to you. If you are evil, evil will be done to you. This is the law of the gods for all eternity.'

Setna bowed his head and let his son lead him out of the Underworld by strange paths. They passed through fire and water and emerged in the western desert again. As they walked back to Memphis, hand in hand, Setna marvelled at the power and wisdom of Sa-Osiris.
'He is almost like a god and yet when people ask me who he is, I can say "This is my son".'

Under his breath, he muttered spells against the demons of the Underworld, for Setna was afraid. He had seen what no living man had seen before and he knew now that even the son of pharaoh must fear the Judgement of the Dead.

The sealed letter

One day the great Pharaoh Ramesses held court at Memphis. As he sat in his throne-room surrounded by princes, generals, councillors, priests and all the great men of Egypt, a Nubian chieftain was announced. Splendid in leopard skin cloak, nodding plumes and bangles of ivory and gold, the tall Nubian strode towards Pharaoh. He bowed three times before the throne but his words were not humble.

'Is there anyone here who can read the letter I carry without opening it? If there is no priest and scribe of your court who is wise enough to read the contents of the letter without breaking the seal and unrolling the papyrus, I shall carry the shame of Egypt back to Nubia!'

The courtiers were astonished and dismayed. None of them had ever heard of a man wise enough to perform such a feat, but Pharaoh said calmly, 'Send for the most learned of my sons, send for Prince Setna Khaemwese.'

A dozen servants ran to fetch the prince and Setna was soon bowing before his father's throne.

'My son,' began Pharaoh, 'this Nubian chieftain demands to know if there is a wise man in Egypt who can read a letter without opening it.'

Setna tried not to let the Nubian see how startled he was. 'This is a foolish request,' he said, 'but give me ten days and I will see what may be done to stop the shame of Egypt being carried to the land of gum-eaters.'

'The days are yours,' answered Pharaoh and he ordered that the chieftain be given comfortable rooms in the palace and servants to cook him Nubian food. Ramesses left the throne-room with great dignity but he could hardly eat or sleep for fear that his country would be shamed.

Setna was in an even worse condition. He wandered back to his house like a sleepwalker and lay down on his bed, hiding his face in his sleeves. Mehusekhe, his wife, hurried to his bedside and put her arms around him.

'My brother, you are cold and shivering. Are you sick or full of grief?'

'Leave me alone,' whispered Setna. 'My heart is grieving over something a woman cannot help me with.'

Then Sa-Osiris came into the bedchamber and asked what the matter was.

'Leave me alone,' muttered Setna. 'You are only twelve and my heart is grieving over something a child cannot help me with.'

'Only tell me what it is,' pleaded Sa-Osiris, 'and I will drive this grief away.'

Then Setna told his son about the Nubian chieftain and his challenge. 'And if I cannot find an Egyptian to read the sealed letter, I and my country will be shamed for ever.'

Sa-Osiris began to laugh and his parent asked him indignantly what was so funny about that. 'O father, I am laughing because you are lying here in despair over so small a matter. I can easily read this Nubian's letter.'

Setna sat up at once but he still could not believe his good fortune. 'Can you prove what you say my son?'

'Go downstairs, father,' answered Sa-Osiris, 'and take a scroll out of one of your book chests. I will read what's in it from the floor above you.'

Setna ran downstairs. He opened a cedar chest and plucked out a roll of papyrus inscribed with spells for healing fevers. He held it up for a minute and then returned to his bedchamber. Sa-Osiris at once began to recite the spells in the scroll, to the delight and amazement of his parents. Again and again Setna ran down to the lower room and held up random scrolls, but Sa-Osiris always knew their contents. Thoroughly convinced, Setna hurried to the palace to tell his father the good news. Ramesses was overjoyed and he invited Setna and his son to spend the night feasting with him.

The next morning, the Nubian chieftain was brought into the throne-room with the sealed letter tied to the belt at his waist. Sa-Osiris stepped forward.

'You fiend of Nubia, you have come to the beautiful land of Egypt, the garden of Osiris, the footstool of Ra, to bring us shame. May Amon strike you down! I shall now read your letter, so do not dare to lie to Pharaoh about its contents.'

'I shall tell no lies,' said the Nubian haughtily. He was not afraid of the mere child who stood before him but his face changed as Sa-Osiris began to speak in a confident voice.

'This is what is written in the Nubian's letter. Many centuries ago, when Pharaoh Siamun ruled Egypt, Nubia was jealous of his wealth and power. One day the Prince of Nubia was resting in the gardens of a temple of Amon when he overheard three sorcerers talking.

"Were it not that Amon and Pharaoh might punish me," said the first sorcerer, "I would cast a spell on Egypt so that the whole land would like in darkness for three days and nights and the people would tremble."

"Were it not that Amon and Pharaoh might punish me," declared the second sorcerer, "I would cast a spell on Egypt so that the whole land would be barren for three years and nothing would grow."

"Were it not that Amon and Pharaoh might punish me," began the third sorcerer, "I would cast a spell on Egypt and fetch Pharaoh to Nubia. I would have him beaten before our Prince and returned to Egypt, all within six hours."

'The prince sent his servants to fetch the three sorcerers and said to them, "Which of you boasted that you could bring Pharaoh here and have him beaten before me?"

"It was Sa-Neheset," answered the other two sorcerers.

"Cast your spell on Egypt," ordered the prince, "and if you succeed, by Amon, the Bull of Meroe, I will do good things for you."

'Sa-Neheset went away and modelled a litter and four bearers out of the finest wax. He recited spells over them and breathed life into them. Then he ordered the bearers to fly to Egypt, bring back Pharaoh to Nubia and give him five hundred blows. The bearers opened their wax mouths and chorused, "We shall do as you say."

'That night the Nubian sorcerer cast his spell against Egypt and the litter-bearers entered the bedchamber of Pharaoh unseen by the guards. They overpowered Siamun with their magic strength, flung him in the litter and carried him back to Nubia. When they reached the prince's palace, Pharaoh was tumbled out and the litter-bearers beat him with sticks while the Nubian court looked on and laughed. Then they returned him to his bed in Egypt, all within six hours. Then the litter-bearers vanished.'

Sa-Osiris paused and there were angry murmurs from the Egyptian courtiers.
'May the anger of Amon strike you if you lie,' threatened the young magician. 'Am I reading your letter?'
'You are,' muttered the Nubian, 'and every word is true.'

Sa-Osiris fixed his eyes on the sealed letter and began again.
'When Siamun found himself in his own bed again, he yelled for his guards and attendants. "How long have I been away," he demanded, "and what has been happening?"
'There was an embarrassed silence. As far as the courtiers knew, Pharaoh had been asleep in his bed all night.
"O Pharaoh, our great lord," began one brave chamberlain, "May Isis heal you! We do not understand you, your Majesty has slept in your Majesty's bed all night."
'Then Siamun turned over and told them to look at his back. "I tell you I was carried to Nubia last night and given five hundred blows."
'When the courtiers saw that Pharaoh's back was dark with bruises they were shocked and horrified and began to wail. No-one knew what to do until the wise magician Sa-Paneshe arrived in the royal bedchamber. He examined Pharaoh and exclaimed, "This is the work of Nubian sorcery and I must turn their magic back against them."
"Hurry," groaned Siamun, "I cannot endure another night like the last one!"
'Sa-Paneshe fetched his amulets and his books of magic. He recited spell after spell over Pharaoh and bound amulets to his brow and neck and arms. Then he left Siamun in the hands of the royal doctors and sailed up river to Hermopolis, to the temple of Thoth. Sa-Paneshe made offerings to the god and prayed aloud, "O great

one, turn your face to me. Do not let Egypt be shamed by Nubia. You are the creator of magic, you know everything that exists on earth and in the sky above and the sky below. Help me to save Pharaoh and defeat the sorcery of Nubia!"

'Then Sa-Paneshe lay down to sleep in the temple. Thoth came to him in a dream and said, "Tomorrow you must search the temple library until you find a secret chamber. Inside the chamber you will find a locked chest and inside the chest a scroll written in my own hand. Take out the Book of Thoth, copy from it the spells you need and return it to its chest. Tell no-one this secret and you will save Pharaoh."

'Sa-Paneshe woke and remembered his dream. He found the scroll and wrote out a mighty spell for the protection of Siamun. That night in Nubia, Sa-Neheset breathed life into his wax figures again and sent them to Egypt. They entered Pharaoh's room unseen but as they approached the bed they seemed to strike an invisible barrier. Siamun felt the amulets he wore throbbing with power and sensed that the spells of Sa-Paneshe were beating back the spells of Nubia. All night long the wax men marched round and round the bed, trying to find a flaw in the magical defences, while Pharaoh lay motionless, hardly daring to breathe. As morning broke, the litter-bearers were forced to fly back to Nubia and Siamun leaped out of bed.

'He summoned Sa-Paneshe and told him everything that had happened. The Egyptian magician was delighted that his spells had worked but he meant to go one step further and punish the Nubians. Sa-Paneshe sent for the purest wax and modelled a litter and four bearers. He breathed life into them and sent them down to Nubia. In the middle of the night they seized the Prince of Nubia, took him back to Egypt and gave him five hundred blows in front of Pharaoh and his court. Then they returned him to his palace, all within six hours.'

Sa-Osiris stopped to ask, 'Is this the truth?' The Nubian's head was bowed in defeat. 'It is.'

'The next morning,' continued Sa-Osiris, 'the Prince of Nubia woke the whole palace with his moans and curses. The sorcerer Sa-Neheset was dragged into his presence and thrown down on the floor beside the bed.

"May the Bull of Meroe curse you," growled the prince. "It was your idea to cast a spell on Egypt. Now save me from this terrible Egyptian sorcerer!"

'Sa-Neheset recited all the protective spells he knew and covered the prince with amulets but that night the wax men came again and took him to Egypt to be beaten. After three nights of this, the anguished prince sent for Sa-Neheset again and said, "By the Bull of Meroe, you have caused me to be humiliated by Egypt. If you cannot save me from their spells tonight I will have you tortured to death!"

'Then Sa-Neheset begged to be allowed to go to Egypt and challenge his rival to a battle of magic. The prince agreed, but before setting out, Sa-Neheset visited his mother, who had taught him most of his magic. When he had told her everything she said to him, "Beware the magicians of Egypt, my son. If you leave Nubia now, surely you will never come back and when we are parted there is nothing I can do to help you."

"I have no choice," answered Sa-Neheset bitterly.

"Then leave me a token," said his mother, "so I will know when you are in danger and need my help."

"If I am defeated by this Egyptian," began Sa-Neheset, "the water you are drinking will turn to the colour of blood and blood will stain the skies."

'Crammed with magic, the Nubian sorcerer hurried to the court at Memphis. He declared himself before Pharaoh and challenged Sa-Paneshe. The two sorcerers stood outside the palace hurling insults at each other, watched by Siamun and his court. Then Sa-Neheset uttered a fire spell and flames burst out of the ground and swept towards Pharaoh. Quicker than thought, Sa-Paneshe had spoken a water spell and sheets of rain extinguished the fire.

'Then Sa-Neheset muttered a spell of darkness. A black cloud enveloped the palace and no-one could see his hand in front of his face. Sa-Paneshe murmured a spell of light and the rays of the sun melted the darkness. Next the Nubian worked a mighty spell and made a huge vault of stone over Pharaoh and his courtiers. The

Egyptians clung together in terror but Sa-Paneshe conjured a giant ship of papyrus and made it carry away the vault and drop it into the sea.

'When Sa-Neheset saw this, he knew that he could never defeat the Egyptian. His only thought was to escape and he made himself invisible and began to creep away. Instantly Sa-Paneshe spoke a spell that made all invisible things visible and Sa-Neheset was exposed. In desperation the Nubian turned himself into a goose and soared upwards. Sa-Paneshe cast a spell to catch him and brought him down on his back with a fowler standing over him with a knife at his throat.

'At that moment, in Nubia, Sa-Neheset's mother saw the water she was drinking turn red and the sky stained with blood. She knew that her son was in terrible danger and she turned herself into a goose and flew to Memphis. There she hovered over the palace, screaming for her son in the voice of a wild bird. Sa-Paneshe recognized her for a sorceress. He spoke another spell and the Nubian woman was soon lying beside her son with a knife at her throat. As she turned back into a woman she begged the Egyptians for mercy.

"If you are to be forgiven," said Sa-Paneshe, "you must swear by all the gods never to come back to Egypt."

'The Nubian woman swore and her son promised that he would not return to Egypt for fifteen hundred years. Pharaoh was satisfied with these oaths and ordered Sa-Paneshe to let the Nubians go. The Egyptian made them a sky boat and together Sa-Neheset and his mother flew back to Nubia and were never seen again.'

Sa-Osiris bowed before Pharaoh. 'Now you have heard the contents of the letter but you do not yet understand why this Nubian has come here. Revenge is the answer. The sorcerer Sa-Neheset has been born again and now that the fifteen hundred years are over he has come here in the form of a chieftain and stands before you!'

There were gasps of amazement from the courtiers but Sa-Osiris swept on. 'He has never repented of his crimes against Egypt and means to do you harm, but he will not succeed for, by Osiris, I am his ancient enemy. I am Sa-Paneshe.

For fifteen hundred years I have lived among the blessed spirits but when I discovered that this fiend of Nubia meant to return to Egypt I begged Osiris to let me be born again and live just long enough to defeat him. Osiris sent my spirit into the melon-vine and I was born to the wife of Setna. So now I stand here to challenge you once more Sa-Neheset!'

When the evil spirit heard these words he began to cast a terrible spell to destroy Pharaoh and his court. Sa-Paneshe countered with a fire spell and the flames surrounded the Nubian sorcerer. Sa-Neheset struggled with spell after spell to hold them back but at last they reached him and consumed him, body and spirit.

Without a word to his father, Sa-Paneshe whom they had known as Sa-Osiris, vanished like a shadow. His task was over and Osiris had summoned him back to the underworld.

Pharaoh and his courtiers began to speak, praising the wisdom of Sa-Paneshe but Setna wept for the loss of his only son. Ramesses tried to comfort him but Setna went back to his house with a sad heart. He lay down on his bed and Mehusekhe lay beside him and they comforted each other. Nine months later another son was born to them, but Setna never ceased to miss Sa-Osiris or to make offerings to his spirit.

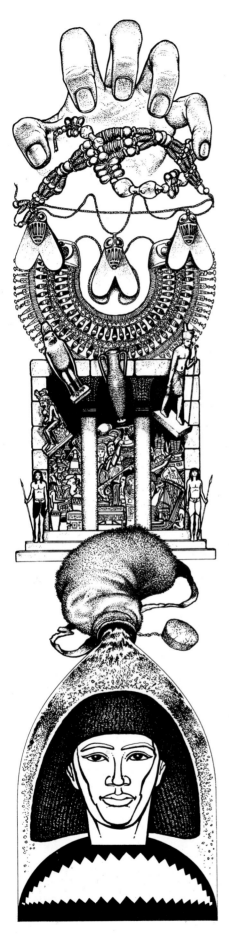

The clever thief

In the fifth century BC a Greek historian called Herodotus visited Egypt. When he came to write about Egypt and its history he included a story about the fabulous treasure of the Pharaoh Rhampsinitus and two thieves who tried to steal it. Rhampsinitus is usually identified with the Pharaoh Ramesses III who ruled Egypt in the twelfth century BC, but no-one is sure how much truth there is in the story. Herodotus is sometimes known as the Father of History, but many people call him the Father of Lies . . .

Rhampsinitus was the richest of all the pharaohs and, to protect his treasure, he ordered the royal architect to build a large room to one side of the palace. This room was to have no windows and only one door and the roof, the floor and the walls were to be built of massive blocks of stone. When the building work was finished Pharaoh filled his new treasury with jars of silver, caskets of jewels and many other precious things. Soldiers were set to guard the door and Rhampsinitus felt quite certain that his treasure was safe.

Several years passed and the royal architect fell ill and soon knew that he was going to die. He called his wife and two sons to his bedside and said to them, 'Pharaoh has never been generous to me and I am not a rich man but I have taken thought for your future. The great stones in the outer wall of the treasury all look the same, but one of them is loose and can easily be moved by two people. I planned this so that my sons could control Pharaoh's treasure.' Then he told them how to find the loose stone but with his last breath warned them not to be too greedy.

Once their father was embalmed and buried, the two brothers lost no time in visiting the treasury. Under cover of darkness, they crept up to the outer wall and quickly found and moved the correct stone. They crept through the gap in the wall and pulled the stone back into place behind them in case anyone came past and raised the alarm. Then they lit the torches they carried with them and gasped at the sight of Pharaoh's treasure.

For an hour the brothers wandered about the treasury, trying on jewelled collars, sniffing rare perfumes and admiring golden statuettes. Finally they remembered the need to get away before dawn. Each of the brothers grabbed two handfuls of silver and they left the treasury by their secret entrance and hurried home.

After this the two brothers visited the treasury night after night. At first they were cautious, taking only small amounts of silver that would hardly be missed and spending their new wealth slowly. Gradually, however, the sight of Pharaoh's glittering treasure inflamed their greed. The brothers forgot their father's warning. They began to take away sackfuls of silver and to steal royal jewels for their mother, jewels that she dared not wear.

One day Rhampsinitus came to his treasury to gloat over his wealth. Pharaoh found the guard alert and the door barred and sealed but when he had broken his own seal and entered the treasury he quickly saw that something was wrong. Some of his favourite jewels were missing and the jars which should have been full to the brim with silver, were half empty. Pharaoh was furiously angry but he was at a loss to know who to blame, since the theft had taken place in a windowless room behind a sealed door.

He ordered that the guard on the treasury should be doubled and resealed the door, but the next morning even more silver had gone from the jars. Pharaoh then had cruel and cunning traps laid in the treasury and waited to see what would happen.

That very night the two brothers moved the stone and crept into the treasury. The elder brother ran eagerly towards the jars of silver and one of the traps closed on him, breaking both his legs. He choked back a shriek of anguish and tried to free himself but the more he struggled the more the teeth of the trap wounded him. His brother tried desperately to free him but with no success. As morning approached, the elder brother knew that he was doomed.
'Brother, either I shall bleed to death before dawn or Pharaoh's guards will find and kill me. If they see my face they will recognize me and our whole family will be punished. Save our mother and yourself and give me a quick death by cutting off my head.'

The younger brother was horrified at being asked to do such a thing but in his heart he knew that he must. He ended his brother's agony with one stroke, severed the head and carried it away

with him, hiding it tenderly under his cloak.

The next morning Pharaoh and his guards entered the treasury and were astounded to find a headless body in one of their traps. There was no sign of how the dead thief had entered the room, so Rhampsinitus was as puzzled as ever. 'The man must have an accomplice,' thought Pharaoh, so he ordered the body to be hung from the outer wall of the palace and set ten men to guard it.
'If you see anyone burst into tears as they pass the body,' said Rhampsinitus, 'arrest them at once!'

The head of the elder brother was lovingly buried by his family but when his mother heard what had happened to the body, she railed at her younger son, 'See where your greed has led us— to misery and disgrace. How can your brother's ka reach the Fields of the Blessed with his head in one place and his body in another?'

She ordered her son to rescue his brother's body and when he refused, threatened to denounce him to Pharaoh as the treasure thief. The younger brother saw that he had no choice and sat down to devise a plan.

The next afternoon he disguised himself and loaded two donkeys with bulging wine-skins. Then he drove the donkeys along the road beside the palace as if he was making for the royal kitchens. He took care not to look up at the pitiful sight of his brother's body hanging on the wall, but when he drew level with the guards he let his donkeys collide, knocking out the stoppers from two of the wine-skins.

The wine gushed out and the younger brother stood dithering in the middle of the road as if he did not know which of the donkeys to cope with first. Seeing good wine going to waste, the soldiers of the guard sprang forward to fill their empty food bowls and flasks. The younger brother swore at them in pretended rage and in a minute or so managed to get the stoppers back into the wine-skins. The guard gathered round him, cracking jokes at his expense, and the younger brother seemed to recover his temper and be so amused that he offered the soldiers one of the half empty wine-skins as a present.

The delighted guards invited him to help them to drink it and they all sat down together in the shadow of the wall. The wine was passed round and the younger brother pretended to drink as much as any of them. Then he got unsteadily to his feet and declared that while they were there, they might as well drink another skinful. The soldiers cheered him and the wine went round again.

It was too much for the guards; first they sang and joked then they quarrelled and cried and finally, one by one, they fell asleep. By this time, dusk had fallen and when the younger brother was sure that all the soldiers were snoring in drunken slumber, he jumped up and cut down his elder brother's body. He slung it over one of the donkeys, covered it with his cloak and took it home. His mother was overjoyed and the body was soon secretly buried in the same tomb as the head.

The next morning the guards woke with terrible headaches; they felt even worse when they saw that the body of the treasure thief had gone. Pharaoh punished them severely and, though he could not help admiring the audacity of the crime, he was more determined than ever to catch the thief.

Rhampsinitus set his daughter up in a house in

the city and promised that she would spend the night with any man who could tell her the most wicked and the most clever things that he had ever done. If anyone told her a story about robbing the treasury, the princess had orders to shout for the soldiers who would be hidden nearby.

The princess was soon the talk of the city and the younger brother could not resist a visit to her, but before he went he stole a dead man's arm from the house of the embalmers and hid it under his cloak. He arrived at the house of the princess after nightfall and was shown into her room. Even by the dim light of a single oil lamp, he could see that she was very beautiful but he sat down on the end of her couch nearest to the door.

When she asked him to hold her hand, the younger brother put out the dead man's hand. The princess took it in hers and said invitingly, 'Tell me the wickedest thing you have ever done and the cleverest, too. Speak the truth and I will be yours.'

'The wickedest thing I ever did was to kill my own brother by cutting off his head,' answered the younger brother, 'but he asked me to do it because he was caught in a trap in the treasury. The cleverest thing I have ever done was to steal my brother's body by making the guards drunk.'

Then the princess knew that she had found the man that Pharaoh was looking for. She shouted out that she had the thief by the hand, but when the soldiers rushed into the room they found the princess in a faint with a severed arm lying beside her on the couch. The younger brother had fled into the night and disappeared.

When Pharaoh heard about this last exploit he decided that it would be better to have such a clever young man as a friend rather than as an enemy. He offered a free pardon and a rich reward if the treasure thief would give himself up. The younger brother trusted the word of Pharaoh and presented himself at the palace and told his whole story. Rhampsinitus rewarded the audacious thief by marrying him to the princess and making him one of his chief councillors. After that, the younger brother never needed to steal again and he put all his cleverness at the service of Pharaoh.

The voyage of Wenamon

By the early eleventh century BC Egypt had lost most of her empire after the mysterious Sea Peoples had invaded from the north and conquered much of Syria and Palestine. In Egypt itself Pharaoh no longer ruled unchallenged and the most powerful man in the south was the high priest of Amon at Thebes. A three-thousand-year-old manuscript claims to relate what happened when the High Priest Herihor sent an envoy to the Lebanon.

Every year the great image of Amon-Ra, King of the Gods, was taken out of the temple and across the Nile to the City of the Dead to feast with Hathor, Lady of Drunkenness. As the years passed the sacred boat which carried the divine image became more and more fragile. The high priest wanted to build a new one but the stunted trees of Egypt could not produce timber of the right length and quality. Only the famous cedars of Lebanon were good enough for such a boat, so Herihor decided to send an envoy to Prince Tjekerbaal who ruled the Lebanon from the city of Byblos. The high priest gathered together enough gold and silver to pay for the costly timber and chose as his envoy a priest called Wenamon. A statuette of Amon of the Road was placed in a gilded shrine and sent with Wenamon to protect him on his journey.

After a swift voyage down the Nile, Herihor's envoy arrived at the city of Tanis and presented himself at the palace of Prince Smendes, who was more powerful in the north than Pharaoh himself. Wenamon handed over a letter written by the high priest on behalf of Amon and a scribe read it aloud to Smendes and his wife, Tentamon. 'We are the servants of the King of the Gods,' said the prince and princess and they promised to find a ship for Wenamon and the men of his escort, and to help his mission in every way they could.

It was two months before a suitable ship could be found but in the fourth month of summer, Wenamon boarded one of Smendes' finest vessels and greeted its Syrian captain, Mengebet. The next day they sailed north and hugged the coast of Palestine until they were forced to put in at the port of Dor to take on fresh supplies. Dor had once been part of the Egyptian empire. Now it belonged to the Tjeker, one of the peoples who had invaded Palestine from the north. Wenamon thought of them as little better than pirates, but he was forced to be polite since he needed their help on his voyage.

Bader, the Tjeker Prince of Dor, sent the Egyptian envoy a gift of fifty loaves, a haunch of roast ox and a jug of strong wine. That night Wenamon and his escort feasted on the deck. The wine was passed round again and again and Wenamon slept where he sat. It was not until morning that anyone noticed that one of the crew had disappeared—and so had all the gold and silver that was to pay for the timber!

Wenamon was distraught. How could he go back to Egypt and confess that the gold and silver had been stolen while he lay drunk on the deck? He hurried to the palace of Beder to see what could be done.

'I have been robbed in your harbour!' began Wenamon. 'You are the ruler here, you are in charge of law and order! Arrest the thief and find my gold and silver. It belongs to Amon-Ra himself and, if it's lost, Smendes and all the nobles of Egypt, the High Priest of Amon and the Prince of Byblos will be angry!'

'Are you joking?' asked Beder coldly. 'What right do you have to come here and give me orders? If the thief had been a Tjeker I would

have replaced your gold and silver from my own treasury. As it is, the thief was one of your own crew, so it's no concern of mine. Nevertheless, as a favour to the King of the Gods, I will order a

thorough search to be made. Stay in harbour for a few days and see if your gold and silver appears.'

Wenamon went back to his ship in a furious temper and waited for nine days. On the tenth day he stormed into the palace and demanded to know if his treasure had been found. Beder simply suggested that he wait a few days longer. Wenamon felt certain that the Tjeker prince had no intention of finding the thief and might even have planned the crime in the first place. He ordered Captain Mengebet to set sail at once.

As they sailed north beyond Dor and past the great port of Tyre, Wenamon brooded on how he could possibly find the price of the timber. Half-way between Tyre and Byblos, they overtook a Tjeker ship. In desperation Wenamon ordered his men to board it and sieze whatever valuables they could find. After a fierce struggle the crew of the smaller ship was overpowered and forced to hand over all the silver they had on board. It came to nearly the same amount that had been stolen in Dor. 'You and your ship are free now,' Wenamon told the outraged Tjeker. 'Go to Beder, your prince and tell him to give you my silver when he finds it.'

Wenamon was feeling very pleased with himself as his ship entered the harbour of Byblos. He set up camp on the sea shore with a special tent for the shrine of Amon of the Road. Captain Mengebet had other commissions from Smendes so the ship sailed on while Wenamon sent a message to Prince Tjekerbaal to say that he had arrived.

It was not long before the master of the harbour approached the Egyptian tents. 'How dare a nobody like you set up camp here?' he demanded. 'The Prince of Byblos orders you to leave his harbour at once.'
'How can I?' asked Wenamon, very taken aback. 'I have no ship, tell your master that.'

The harbour master repeated Wenamon's words to the prince but the curt message came back, 'Get out of my harbour!'

Every day the Egyptian envoy asked to see the prince and every day he was refused.
'Well if you want me to go,' said Wenamon angrily, 'give me a ship.'
'Get out of my harbour!' was the only answer.

After a month of this humiliation, Wenamon was ready to give up. When he discovered that there was a Syrian ship in harbour willing to take passengers for Egypt, he ordered his men to start packing. By the middle of the afternoon only the tent of Amon of the Road was still standing. Wenamon could not bear the thought of foreigners staring at the shrine and mocking the god, so he decided to wait until dusk before carrying Amon of the Road aboard the Syrian ship.

That same afternoon, Prince Tjekerbaal had gone to the chief temple of Byblos. As he approached the altar of the goddess of Byblos, carrying a dish of smouldering incense, one of his pages fell down in a fit. The boy turned white, his limbs shook, his head lolled and he spoke in a deep voice that was not his own. Everyone could see that he had been possessed by some god and they crowded round him to catch his words.
'Bring up Amon of the Road,' gasped the boy. 'Summon the envoy who is with him. The King of the Gods has sent this man. See him, listen to him!'

Then the boy fainted and as priests and courtiers clustered round, trying to revive him, Tjekerbaal began to wonder if he had made a mistake in ignoring Wenamon. He knew that the troublesome envoy was due to leave that night so he sent a messenger racing down to the harbour.

Just as Wenamon was going into the tent to fetch the shrine of Amon of the Road, the Harbour Master ran up to him calling, 'Don't leave! The prince orders you to stay until morning.'
'Are my eyes failing me or are you the same man who has come to me every morning saying, "Go away! Leave my harbour!"' mimicked Wenamon. 'This is just a trick. You want me to miss my only chance of getting home and then tomorrow you'll come again to say "Go away" and blame everything on me.'

However much the harbour master protested that it was not a trick, Wenamon refused to believe him and went on packing. When Tjekerbaal heard this he ordered the Syrian ship to stay in harbour as a token of his good faith to Wenamon. Reluctantly, Wenamon stayed on.

The next morning messengers arrived to escort the Egyptian envoy through the city of Byblos to the palace of Tjekerbaal. Wenamon knelt before the shrine of Amon of the Road to pray for courage and a clever tongue and then let the messengers take him to their prince.

Tjekerbaal received him in an upper room overlooking the great harbour. The prince sat in an ivory chair with his back to the window so that the waves seemed to break against his head. He wore a robe of costly Tyrian purple and golden rings on every plump finger. Wenamon bowed and said grandly, 'I bring you the blessing of Amon-Ra, King of the Gods.'

'And when did you leave the holy place of Amon?' asked the prince.

'Five months ago,' Wenamon answered promptly.

'If this is true,' said Tjekerbaal, 'do you have a letter from the High Priest of Amon to prove that you are who you say you are?'

'I did have a letter,' muttered Wenamon, 'but I gave it to Smendes.'

Tjekerbaal lost his temper. 'I see; so you arrive at my palace with no ship and no letter, expecting me to do what ever you say, and you don't even claim to come from Pharaoh! Smendes probably sent you off in a Syrian ship to get rid of you, hoping the captain would throw you overboard!'

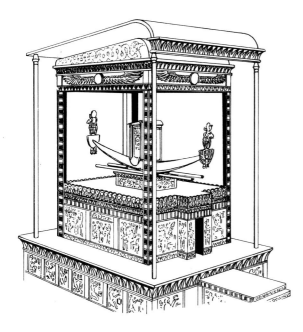

'It was not a Syrian ship,' protested Wenamon. 'It was an Egyptian ship because the crew serve Smendes.'

'Well, well,' said Tjekerbaal irritably, 'what is your business?'

Wenamon came nearer the prince, until there was only the width of an ebony table between them.

'I have come for timber to rebuild the sacred boat of the great god Amon. You know that your father and your father's father sent timber to Egypt. It is your duty to do the same.'

'I'll send timber to Egypt, when Egypt can pay for it,' snapped Tjekerbaal. 'It's true that my ancestors traded with your pharaohs but they didn't cut cedars for them until six Egyptian ships had unloaded their goods onto the quay at Byblos. If you don't believe me, look at the accounts.'

The prince sent for them and three scribes came in, staggering under the weight of piles of yellowing scrolls. Tjekerbaal picked up one that dated to his great-grandfather's day and read out the list of goods supplied by Pharaoh in return for timber for boat-building. Feeling more and more discouraged, Wenamon listened with bowed head.

'If the ruler of Egypt was my overlord,' continued the prince, 'he would simply order me to cut the timber with no talk of payment, but he is not and he cannot. I am not your servant and I am not the servant of the ones who sent you! I am the Lord of the Lebanon. When I speak the cedars fall and the logs lie on the shore. Where is your ship to carry the logs home? Where are the ropes to lash your logs to the deck? Must I do everything for you? It is true that Amon made Egypt before all other lands and that wisdom and skill came to Byblos from Egypt, but that was long ago. Egypt is no-one's master now. You have made a pointless journey.'

Anger lent Wenamon boldness. 'You are wrong. There is no ship that sails on river or sea that doesn't belong to Amon and as for this Lebanon that you call yours, it is nothing but a timber yard for the King of the Gods! How dare you haggle over the price of timber with the envoy of your god? Pharaohs in the past may have sent you shiploads of gold but I can offer you divine gifts. If you say "Yes" to Amon, he will reward you with long life and health.'

Wenamon paused for a moment and then said, 'If you are still doubtful, let me dictate a letter to Smendes and Tentamon, the true servants of Amon. They will repay you for the full expense of cutting and shipping the timber.'

Tjekerbaal was obviously more impressed by the promise of trade goods from Egypt than by divine blessings. One of the scribes stepped forward and the letter was quickly dictated.

Wenamon set up his camp again on the seashore and waited hopefully. After several months, messengers arrived from Egypt. They brought five jars of gold and five of silver, garments woven of the finest linen, five hundred mats, five hundred ropes and five hundred ox-hides for Tjekerbaal. In addition, the Princess Tentamon had sent new clothes, a sack of lentils and five baskets of dried fish for Wenamon.

The prince was delighted with the Egyptian goods and assigned three hundred men to start cutting the timber. The great cedars were felled and left to mature all winter. Then the trunks were stripped of their branches, cut up into logs and dragged by oxen to the seashore.

In the third month of summer, Tjekerbaal sent for the Egyptian envoy. The prince was walking in the palace gardens, protected by a sun-shade and surrounded by fawning courtiers. Many of them were Egyptians who had deserted their own country for the rich court of Byblos and they mocked poor Wenamon until Tjekerbaal said, 'Well, the last of your timber is ready and I have supplied the ships and crews to carry it to Egypt, even though the payment was small. Since you ought to fear my anger more than a storm at sea, set sail at once. I trust that you are grateful. After all, I might have done to you what was done by my father to the envoys of the Vizier Khaemwese. They spent seventeen years waiting in Byblos. Would you like to see their graves?'

'There will be no need,' said Wenamon nervously. 'The vizier was only a man and his envoys were only men. I am the envoy of a god.

You should inscribe on stone, for all men to see, that you welcomed the envoy of Amon, graciously gave him ships and timber and sent him back to Egypt to ask the god for fifty extra years of life for you.'

'These are fine words,' said Tjekerbaal dryly.

'When I get home,' answered Wenamon, 'I shall tell the god and his high priest everything which you have done and they will reward you accordingly.'

The envoy of Egypt bowed to the Prince of Byblos and walked down to the harbour overjoyed that his difficult mission was nearly over. Then he noticed that the harbour was full of Tjeker ships. A Tjeker captain standing on the quay saw Wenamon and shouted, 'That's the man who stole our silver! Arrest him, don't let his ships sail to Egypt!'

Wenamon sat down with his head in his hands and almost wept with frustration. One of Tjekerbaal's scribes hurried up to him to ask what was the matter.

'What is it?'

Wenamon looked up. 'Do you see those birds overhead? They are flying down from Byblos to winter in the warmth of Egypt. They will be there long before me and perhaps I shall never see my home again. Those Tjeker pirates have come to arrest me.'

The scribe ran to the palace to tell his prince what had happened. Tjekerbaal was very annoyed. Now that he had cut the timber for Wenamon he did not want the deal to fall through at the last minute.

'Tell the Tjeker and the Egyptian envoy that I will judge between them in the morning,' said the prince. Secretly, he sent a second message to Wenamon, telling him not to despair. With the message arrived two jugs of the best wine, a whole sheep and a beautiful Egyptian singer who usually waited on Tjekerbaal himself.

Wenamon tried to be cheerful. He had the sheep roasted and shared the wine with the singing girl. Then they sat together on the seashore, the girl playing her harp and singing Egyptian love songs and Wenamon staring at the waves and thinking longingly of home.

In the morning the Tjeker put their case against Wenamon before the Prince of Byblos

and his court. Tjekerbaal pretended to listen with great sympathy.

'And what is it that you want me to do?'

'Arrest him for us,' said the Tjeker captain, 'and let us take him back to Dor to face the punishment for theft.'

'If this Egyptian were only a man, serving an earthly ruler I would hand him to you with pleasure, but alas,' sighed Tjekerbaal, 'he is the envoy of the King of the Gods. As a devout worshipper of Amon, how could I commit the terrible crime of detaining his envoy?'

The Tjeker began to mutter angrily but the prince continued. 'What I shall do is this. The Egyptian will go down to his ships and set sail. As soon as he is out of the harbour of Byblos, I shall release you and your ships so that you can chase him. If you catch him on the open sea that is not my affair and the god cannot blame me.'

The prince was very pleased with this solution, since once Wenamon had left Byblos with the timber, Smendes could not demand the payment back. The Tjeker had to be content with it, too, and Wenamon ran for the harbour. He gathered up the last of his luggage and ordered his captains to sail and put on all the speed they could. Heavily laden with timber, his ships were not as light and swift as those of the Tjeker and Wenamon knelt on the deck and prayed to Amon of the Roads for help.

As soon as they had rowed out of the harbour a strong wind sprang up, blowing them towards Egypt. Wenamon leaned against the mast, limp with relief. Within half an hour they sighted the sails of the Tjeker ships but with such a strong wind behind them there was a good chance that they could keep ahead. Gradually the sky darkened and the wind blew stronger. Lightning flashed, rain sheeted down and the Egyptian ships were soon too busy struggling to survive the storm, to worry about the Tjeker.

The storm raged all through the night but at dawn they sighted land and the weary captains made straight for the shelter of the nearest harbour. The Tjeker had been left far behind, but Wenamon soon had a new worry. His captains assured him that they must have reached the island of Alasiya, the realm of the Princess Hatiba, but the local people seemed far from

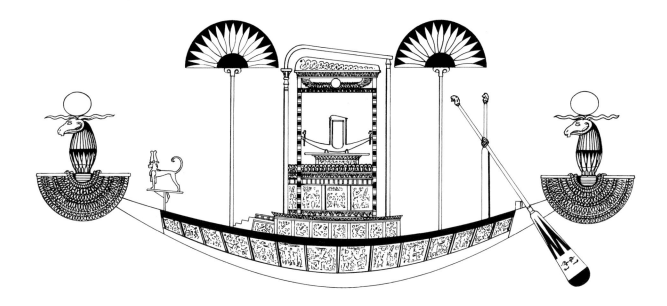

friendly. They were gathering on the quay in an angry crowd and some of them were armed with swords and bows.

Afraid that the townspeople might be about to attack his ships, Wenamon decided to go ashore and look for someone in authority. Surrounded by six of his stoutest men, Wenamon walked down the gangplank into the hostile crowd. At first they were only jostled and jabbered at but then someone threw a stone. Wenamon put up a hand to protect himself but the crowd took it as a threatening gesture and attacked. The Egyptians drew their daggers and prepared to fight for their lives.

Just at that moment, the Princess Hatiba herself came out of a nearby house to see what the commotion was about. Wenamon threw himself at her feet and said desperately, 'Isn't there anyone here who understands Egyptian?' 'I understand it,' said one of Hatiba's attendants. 'Who are you?'
'Tell your lady that I am Wenamon, the envoy of the great god Amon. I come from Thebes, the holy city of Amon and even there we have heard that justice reigns in Alasiya. But is it just to attack someone who has been driven into your harbour by a storm? The crews of my ships belong to the great Prince of Byblos and if anything happened to them here he would be very angry and take his revenge.'

When all this had been translated for the princess she ordered her people to lay down their arms and scolded them for attacking innocent strangers. Then she smiled at the Egyptian envoy and spoke to him in her own language.
'My lady asks you to spend the night in her palace,' said the interpreter and Wenamon accepted gratefully.

For two days and nights Wenamon and his men enjoyed the hospitality of Hatiba. She urged him to stay longer but Wenamon was afraid that the Tjeker might yet catch up with him, so he left Alasiya on the third morning, loaded with gifts for Amon. The captains took a different route from the outward voyage but Wenamon was always nervously watching the horizon for Tjeker sails. He did not feel safe until they reached the coast of Egypt and the timber was taken off and loaded into barges for the long slow journey up the Nile.

Wenamon called at Tanis to thank Smendes and Tentamon for the goods they had sent to Byblos. Then he rejoined the barges and a month later he was back in Thebes. The whole city rejoiced to see the timbers arrive at last. A magnificent boat was built for the image of Amon-Ra, and the high priest rewarded Wenamon and thanked the gods for his safe return to the land of his birth.

Egypt in decline

In spite of the grandiose splendour of Ramesses II's reign, Egypt's power was already waning. The late second millenium BC was a time of turmoil in the Near East; old empires were breaking up and new countries, like Israel, were being formed. At first this turmoil must have seemed remote to Egypt but the successors of Ramesses II soon had to defend their borders against foreign enemies. Libyan tribes, intent on settling in the Delta, attacked from the west and from the north came invasions by the mysterious Sea Peoples who had already swept away the mighty Hittite empire. In the reign of Ramesses III (c1194–1163 BC), the Sea Peoples were defeated in two great battles, one on land and one at sea. Egypt was saved, but most of her empire and with it much of her prosperity, had gone for ever. The story of 'The voyage of Wenamon' shows how low Egypt's prestige had sunk by the eleventh century BC.

Ramesses III was followed by a series of weak pharaohs and the government became corrupt and inefficient. The craftsmen of Deir el-Medina went on strike several times because their wages had not been paid and there was a major scandal when it came out that the authorities in Thebes had been turning a blind eye to the robbery of ancient royal tombs. Nubia slipped out of Egypt's grasp and the leaders of the army and the priesthood became more and more powerful and founded dynasties of their own.

When the line of Ramesses died out, a new dynasty, the Twenty-First (c1070–945 BC), ruled from the city of Tanis in the Delta, but the unity of Egypt was growing frailer. The next dynasty was of Libyan descent and soon split into two rival branches. By the eighth century BC Egypt was divided amongst half a dozen rulers, all claiming to be kings. These petty kings were all defeated in 730 BC by Piye of Napata, the ruler of Nubia. Though Nubia had been independent for centuries, the kings of Napata were in many ways more Egyptian than the Egyptians. They were devoted to the god Amon and still had themselves buried in pyramids, though the custom had died out in Egypt a thousand years before. King Piye's descendants reunited Egypt and ruled as the Twenty-Fifth Dynasty (c712–657 BC). The last of these Nubian kings was driven back to Napata by an Assyrian invasion.

From their capital of Niniveh, the Assyrians had conquered a huge empire and were infamous for the cruelty of their rule. The invasion was a terrible blow to Egyptian pride but the Assyrians did not have enough troops to subdue Egypt completely. They were forced to rule through Egyptian vassals, who were supposed to pay tribute to the Assyrian king. One of these vassals, Psammetichus of Sais, soon led a successful revolt against the Assyrians and claimed the throne of all Egypt. He and his dynasty, the Twenty-Sixth, ruled a united country from 664 to 525 BC.

The Twenty-Sixth Dynasty was a time of comparative peace and prosperity for Egypt. The only threat came from King Nebuchadnezzar of Babylon who had captured Jerusalem and carried the Jews into exile, but his attacks on Egypt were all defeated. In the late sixth century BC, Persia replaced Assyria and Babylon as the greatest power in the Near East and in 525 BC the Persian king, Cambyses, successfully invaded Egypt.

In the fourth century BC Egyptian leaders struggled to make their country independent again. For a time they were successful but the Persians soon reconquered Egypt and ruled more oppressively than ever before. Then the Persian empire itself came under attack from the young King of Macedonia, Alexander the Great. In 332 BC Alexander drove the Persians out of Egypt and was hailed by his new subjects as the son of Amon.

When Alexander died, in 323 BC, his body was brought to Egypt and buried, first at Memphis, and then in a splendid tomb in the new city of Alexandria. His vast empire was divided amongst his generals and Egypt became the share of General Ptolemy, whose descendants ruled the country for the next two hundred and fifty years. Alexandria, with its famous library, became a great centre of Greek learning and Greek law and coinage were introduced, but the Egyptians were allowed to go on building temples to their gods. These acted as strongholds of their ancient culture.

As a family the Ptolemies were cruel and quarrelsome and the women were as ruthless as the men. The most famous of the Ptolemies, Queen Cleopatra VII, had already killed an elder sister and was fighting a war against her younger brother when Julius Caesar arrived in Egypt in 48 BC. To save his throne during a revolt, Cleopatra's father had put Egypt under Roman protection and Rome was only waiting for an excuse to make the country part of her growing empire.

Cleopatra kept Egypt independent by winning Caesar's favour and she bore him his only son. When Julius Caesar was murdered, his power was divided between his friend Mark Antony and his great-nephew Octavian. Antony took charge of the eastern empire and one of his first tasks was to demand the homage of Egypt. However, when Cleopatra came, the Roman general was dazzled by her. Antony and Cleopatra were soon ruling the east together from Alexandria, careless of the disapproval of Rome; but when the inevitable clash with Octavian came they were quickly defeated. Rather than be forced to walk in chains through the streets of Rome, both Antony and Cleopatra killed themselves.

So in 30 BC Egypt became a mere province of the Roman empire. Like the Greeks before them, the new conquerors were fascinated by Egyptian culture. A religion which promised a happy afterlife had a great appeal to the Romans and the cults of Isis and Osiris spread across the empire. A temple of Isis was even built in England, in the Roman city of Londinium. It was not the rule of Rome but the rise of Christianity which was to destroy Egypt's ancient culture. When Christianity became the official religion of the Roman empire, the temples of Egypt were forced to close. Ancient tombs became the homes of Christian hermits, the images of the old gods were defaced and the meaning of the hieroglyphic inscriptions was forgotten. The Egyptians deliberately turned away from their past.

In the seventh century AD Egypt was invaded by the Arabs and became a brilliant centre of Islamic civilization, but a large Christian community remained. The language of this community was Coptic, a mixture of Greek and Egyptian. Still used in the services of the Coptic church, it provides the last living link with the culture of Ancient Egypt.

Writing in Ancient Egypt

Writing was first used in Egypt in about three thousand BC. From that time onwards the country was governed by people who had been trained as scribes and who could read and write the Egyptian language. Reed brushes were used for writing and every scribe carried a palette with cakes of red and black ink, a water pot and a tool for smoothing the surface of paper. Egyptian paper was made from the beaten pith of papyrus stems. It was an expensive material and rough work or school exercises were written on flakes of limestone or potsherds (pieces of broken pottery) instead.

For most of Egyptian history there were two main scripts: hieroglyphic and hieratic. The beautiful hieroglyphic script with its detailed pictures of men, objects and animals was carved or painted on stelae and statues or in tombs or temples but rarely written on papyrus. For everyday use there were simplified or abbreviated hieroglyphs, which made up the flowing hieratic script. Both scripts were usually written from right to left with no breaks between words or sentences and no punctuation marks.

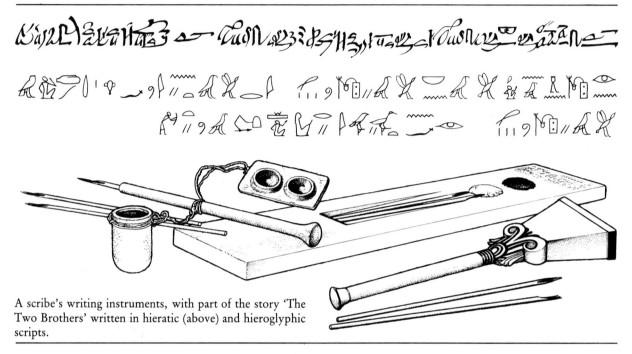

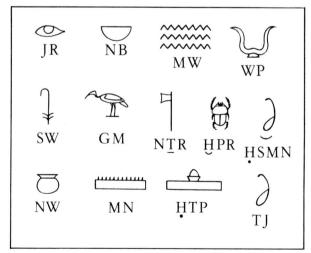

A scribe's writing instruments, with part of the story 'The Two Brothers' written in hieratic (above) and hieroglyphic scripts.

HIEROGLYPHIC SCRIPT

The hieroglyphic script is often referred to as 'picture-writing' but this is misleading. The seven hundred hieroglyphs that were in general use can be divided into two types of sign: phonograms and semograms. Phonograms represent sounds and semograms convey the meaning of whole words. The most common phonograms were twenty-four signs which represent a single consonant or semi-vowel such as:

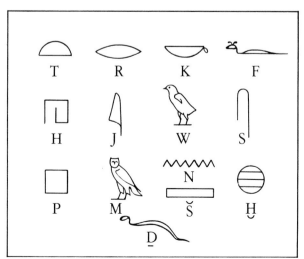

Other signs each represented a combination of between two and four sounds:

As in many oriental languages, vowels were not written down. This makes it very difficult to decide how an ancient Egyptian word was pronounced or how it should be written out in full. Scholars following different systems often spell the same word in a variety of ways, so that the god of Thebes may be written as Amon, Amun or Amen.

To add to the confusion, early Egyptologists frequently used ancient Greek versions of Egyptian words and the Greek names for most Egyptian towns. Names such as Thoth or Hermopolis are now so well known that they have to be preferred to the Egyptian.

In addition to the phonograms two types of semogram were used, logograms and taxograms. Logograms indicate the meaning of a whole word by an appropriate picture:

 writes bull  writes scribe

Taxograms were written at the end of a word and they show the general area of meaning to which the word belongs. Verbs of motion, such as to go or to walk, end with a pair of legs:

 to go   to walk

Words to do with light often end with a picture of the disc or of the sun:

 day   shine

Proper names end with a seated male or female figure:

Amonhotep   Tentamon

Most Egyptian words are made up of a mixture of phonograms and taxograms:

 rm (fish) is written with an *r* sign, an *m* sign and a picture of a fish.

 jnr (stone) is written with a *j* sign, an *n* sign, an *r* sign and a block of stone.

In some words a single sound is expressed twice by different types of phonogram:

hnw (praise or rejoicing) is written with an *h* sign, an *n* sign, an *nw* sign, a *w* sign and a taxogram of a man kneeling beating his chest. It should be read as *hnw* not *hnnww*, since the *n* sign and the *w* sign simply reinforce the meaning of the *nw* sign.

To make matters more complicated some signs can act as phonograms, logograms and taxograms:

 spells *pr* in some words.

 But because its sign is a simplified house plan it can also be used as a logogram to write house.

 It can also be used as a taxogram in words connected with building such as *mnw* (fortress).

This, together with the Egyptian habit of rearranging the signs to make a word look neater, can make a text from ancient Egypt very hard to decipher. Excavating temples and tombs may be more exciting but it is the dedicated scholars who have struggled to understand the Egyptian language who are the true heroes of Egyptology.

Symbols in the Egyptian myths

At the beginning of each chapter the artist has illustrated some of the objects and symbols identified with the characters and events of the story.

p. 11 RED LAND, BLACK LAND Typical images of ancient Egypt. From the top: the pyramids at Giza, the combined red and white crown of the Two Lands, an early Egyptian community, the outer case of a coffin containing a mummy, the craftsman's village of Deir el-Medina, the River Nile.

p. 21 THE NINE GODS At the top, a stylized representation of the sky goddess Nut and, at the bottom, of the earth god Geb. The central figure is Ra-Atum and the board and pieces are for the Egyptian version of draughts. The birds are ibises, sacred to Thoth.

p. 24 THE SECRET NAME OF RA The Sun God, Ra, is drawn in Egyptian style as a man with a scarab beetle for a head. The magic snake is shown threatening Ra and crumbling into dust after biting him.

p. 26 THE EYE OF THE SUN At the top the sun covered in gloom symbolizes Egypt's depression. Hathor as wildcat looks down on scenes from three of the fables Thoth relates. Below, Thoth as a baboon.

p. 34 THE ANGER OF RA The Sun God shines down on Egypt, shown first as prosperous and then empty of human inhabitants. Nut, in her cow form, wears a sun disc, uraeus serpent and double plume between her horns. At the bottom, Hathor in her lioness form.

p. 36 THE MURDER OF OSIRIS The Nile flowing into the sea forms the background. Isis, as a swallow, circles the tree-pillar which hides the body of Osiris. Below, the infant Horus in the marshes.

p. 41 THE CONFLICT OF HORUS AND SETH Falcon-headed Horus wearing the white crown, with above, the pine boat he used to trick Seth and, below, the two gods fighting as hippopotami.

p. 48 THE JOURNEY OF THE SOUL A wrapped mummy is surrounded by its *ka*. Above is the *ba* or soul, in the form of a heron. Behind is the doorway to the Underworld with, below, the ass-eating serpents and the fire, symbolizing the ordeals through which the *ba* had to pass. At the base, a vessel for embalming fluid in the form of a lotus, a symbol of rebirth.

p. 51 THE SEVEN YEAR FAMINE The ram-headed god Khnum releases the Nile onto a drought-stricken Egypt.

p. 53 KING KHUFU AND THE MAGICIANS At the top, the wax crocodile becomes a real one. In the centre one of King Sneferu's rowers and her fish-shaped pendant. At the bottom, the goose, duck and ox whose severed heads were rejoined to their bodies by the magician Djedi.

p. 60 THE ELOQUENT PEASANT Scenes from daily life based on wall paintings: woman and child gathering grain; the making of bread and beer; peasant and loaded donkey; and scribe with scrolls and writing instruments. In the centre, the peasant pleading his case against the corrupt official.

p. 64 THE SHIPWRECKED SAILOR The giant serpent looms over the sailor and the fruits of the mysterious island. Below, a fire drill.

p. 69 THE CAPTURE OF JOPPA Egyptian war chariot and arms (bronze scimitar and poleaxe weighted with ball). Below stylized drawing of walled city and symbols of encampment and soldiers carrying a basket.

p. 71 THE DOOMED PRINCE The prince and his fates—crocodile, snake and dog with the water demon and the tower in which the princess was confined.

p. 77 THE TWO BROTHERS The wives of the two brothers are enclosed in stylized hearts. At top and bottom are cedar and persea trees. Between the figures are small sarcophagi, symbolizing the deaths of the two faithless women.

p. 84 THE BLINDING OF TRUTH Lies (top) gloats over Truth's disgrace. Below, Truth is discovered by Desire's maidservants, then slumps in despair at her door. Bottom, Truth reaches up for justice.

p. 86 THE SUN PHARAOH At the top, Akhenaten, wearing the double crown and below, the bust of Nefertiti from el-Amarna. In the centre, the Aten (solar disc) with rays ending in hands holding out the sign of life.

p. 88 THE PRINCESS OF BAKHTAN The god Khons, holding a crook and flail and wearing the sidelock that symbolizes childhood and the disc of the full moon.

p. 92 THE BOOK OF THOTH The prince and his brother approach the inner chamber of the tomb.

p. 103 THE YOUNG MAGICIAN Osiris, in feathered crown, sits beneath a golden canopy with a lotus flower and jackal-headed Anubis and ibis-headed Thoth before him. In the centre, the scales weigh the heart of a dead man against the feather of Truth and the Devourer waits to snatch the damned. Below, father and son fall into the Underworld past the guardian demons.

p. 108 THE SEALED LETTER The Nubian chieftain with his sealed papyrus scroll. Above, the sorcerer's mother in her goose form. Below, the sorcerer returns to Egypt for revenge.

p. 114 THE CLEVER THIEF A thieving hand grasps typical Egyptian gold and silver jewelry. Below, a stylized treasure room, and a wineskin from which wine pours over a sculpture of a severed head. Bottom, the teeth of a man-trap.

p. 117 THE VOYAGE OF WENAMON Wenamon's ships are caught in a storm; below, the cedars of Lebanon.

p. 126 EGYPT IN DECLINE The crumbling majesty of ancient Egypt, based on a statue of Zoser, and coins showing Alexander and Ptolemy I. In the centre, Cleopatra VII, Julius Caesar and Mark Antony. Below, the step-pyramid of Zoser forms the background to the newer influences of Christianity and Islam, symbolized by the cross and the hand. The fingers of the hand represent the five pillars of Islam and the script reads 'God is great'.

Index

Figures in italics refer to illustrations